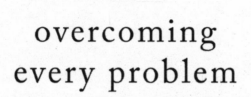

overcoming
every problem

overcoming
every problem

40 PROMISES FROM GOD'S WORD TO STRENGTHEN YOU THROUGH LIFE'S GREATEST CHALLENGES

JOYCE MEYER

FaithWords

New York • Nashville

Copyright © 2023 by Joyce Meyer

Cover copyright © 2023 by Hachette Book Group, Inc.

Hachette Book Group supports the right to free expression and the value of copyright. The purpose of copyright is to encourage writers and artists to produce the creative works that enrich our culture.

The scanning, uploading, and distribution of this book without permission is a theft of the author's intellectual property. If you would like permission to use material from the book (other than for review purposes), please contact permissions@hbgusa.com. Thank you for your support of the author's rights.

FaithWords
Hachette Book Group
1290 Avenue of the Americas, New York, NY 10104
faithwords.com
twitter.com/faithwords

First Edition: May 2023

FaithWords is a division of Hachette Book Group, Inc. The FaithWords name and logo are trademarks of Hachette Book Group, Inc.

The publisher is not responsible for websites (or their content) that are not owned by the publisher.

The Hachette Speakers Bureau provides a wide range of authors for speaking events. To find out more, go to www.hachettespeakersbureau.com or call (866) 376-6591.

Library of Congress Cataloging-in-Publication Data
Names: Meyer, Joyce, 1943- author.
Title: Overcoming every problem : 40 promises from God's word to strengthen you through life's greatest challenges / Joyce Meyer.
Description: First edition. | New York, NY : FaithWords, 2023.
Identifiers: LCCN 2022053151 | ISBN 9781546029151 (hardcover) | ISBN 9781546004653 (large print) | ISBN 9781546029144 (ebook)
Subjects: LCSH: Trust in God--Christianity. | Spiritual life--Christianity.
Classification: LCC BV4637 .M447 2023 | DDC 242/.2--dc23/eng/20230123
LC record available at https://lccn.loc.gov/2022053151

ISBNs: 978-1-5460-2915-1 (hardcover), 978-1-5460-0465-3 (large print), 978-1-5460-2914-4 (ebook)

Printed in the United States of America

LSC-C

Printing 1, 2023

Contents

Introduction

God's Word, the Bible, has helped me overcome many problems and has changed my life and the lives of millions of other people. Jesus is the Word made flesh who came to dwell on earth, among us (John 1:14). He came to save us from our sins and to give us an abundant life filled with every blessing we can imagine (Matthew 1:21; John 10:10). I always knew Jesus died to save me from my sins, but I was not aware that He also died for me to have an abundant life, a life I could enjoy.

God's Word does many things for us if we study it, believe it, and apply it to our lives. People are destroyed because they lack knowledge (Hosea 4:6). I have studied God's Word for more than forty years, and it has been the best investment of time I could have made. I am amazed at what I did not know in my early years as a Christian and therefore could not apply to my life. I went to church each week in those days, but I did not study God's Word for myself. Spending time on our own studying God's Word is necessary for us to grow in our faith. Hearing others teach God's Word is important too, but studying it for ourselves is what plants it deeply in our hearts.

I had a lot of dysfunctional behavior in my life due to being sexually abused by my father and abandoned to the abuse by my mother, but God has healed my wounded soul through the power of His Word. Perhaps you have also been hurt in various ways. No matter what has caused your pain or how deep the wounds may be, I can assure you that God will also heal you and teach you how to be an overcomer in life if you ask Him to and apply His Word to your life. John 8:31–32 says that if we continue in God's Word, we will know the truth and the truth will make us free. However, just reading it doesn't make us free; we must apply it and do what it instructs us to do.

One good example is the subject of forgiving those who have hurt us. Jesus says we must forgive our enemies, pray for them, and bless them (Matthew 5:44; Luke 6:27–28). This seems to be unfair, and it is difficult emotionally, so most people simply don't do it. Someone who has hurt you may not deserve your forgiveness, but you deserve peace. Forgiving them will give you peace. Many people are filled with bitterness, resentment, and unforgiveness, which opens a door for their enemy, Satan, to enter their lives and bring destruction. They may be familiar with the Word, but because they are not willing to apply it, it won't bring the freedom and healing that they need.

God always shows us what to do, and He gives us the strength and courage to do it. However, we still have to act on it. He will not force us to do things His way, because He has given us free will. My prayer is that as you see in this book all the wonderful things God's Word promises to do for you, you will want to study it and apply it to your life. If you do, I can promise you that you will never be sorry.

> For everyone born of God overcomes the world. This is the victory that has overcome the world, even our faith. Who is it that overcomes the world? Only the one who believes that Jesus is the Son of God.
>
> 1 John 5:4–5

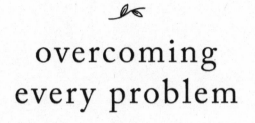

overcoming
every problem

1

⸙

God's Word
teaches truth

⸙

*To the Jews who had believed him, Jesus said,
"If you hold to my teaching, you are really
my disciples. Then you will know the truth,
and the truth will set you free."*

John 8:31–32

Jesus is the Word made flesh who came to earth to dwell among us (John 1:14). He says that He is the truth (John 14:6). God's Word teaches us truth, and if we do not know His Word, Satan, the deceiver, can easily deceive us. He will be able to lie to us, and we will believe his lies because we do not know the truth.

If we believe a lie, the lie becomes our reality, because we don't know it is not true. For example, if we believe we cannot do something, we will not be able to do it even if we are actually capable of doing it. It is vital for us to know the truth, and absolute truth can only be found in the Word of God.

Satan deceived Eve in the Garden of Eden (Genesis 3:13) and has been deceiving people since then. He convinced Eve that God didn't really mean what she thought He meant when He told her not to eat of the fruit of the tree of the knowledge of good and evil (Genesis 2:17; 3:1–5). Through believing his lies, she gave him access to her life and an opportunity to destroy all the good things God intended for her. Being deceived is not an excuse for disobedience because we have a responsibility to know God's Word. And if we do not know it, we will be deceived.

We have a responsibility
to know God's Word.

Eve not only sinned personally but also gave some of the forbidden fruit to Adam, and he ate it in disobedience to God. God corrected Adam, Eve, and Satan, but thankfully He also had a plan for Adam and Eve's redemption. His plan was to send Jesus (the truth) to pay for their sin and all sin that would ever be committed by any person.

When we know and apply the truth of God's Word to our lives, it sets us free from the bondage that Satan's lies have created in our lives. Jesus came to set us free, and those whom the Son sets free are "free indeed" (John 8:36).

The world we live in today is confusing, and

knowing what the truth is can be challenging. We encounter lies everywhere we turn. But thankfully we have a source of truth that will always guide us in the right direction: God's Word, the Bible. God's Word is our source of truth, and studying it is the wisest thing we can do.

Isaiah 5:20 says, "Woe to those who call evil good and good evil." We are living in a time when people are doing just that. These are dangerous days, days when many people no longer know the truth and are susceptible to Satan's lies.

Invest time each day in studying the truth of God's Word, and it will always guide you in the right direction. It will cause you to recognize Satan's lies and avoid being deceived by them. Teach the Word of God to your children, and let it guide your family life. It is important to teach your children the Word and to be an example to them of someone who applies God's Word to their life.

Just as we need food for our physical bodies, we also need food for our spirit and soul. God's Word is the food that we need. In Matthew 4:4, Jesus says that people do not live "by bread alone, but by every word that proceeds from the mouth of God" (NKJV).

The words God speaks are "full of the Spirit and life" (John 6:63). The flesh profits nothing, but God's Word ministers life to us—not just natural life, but life as God has it. I want this life, and I'm sure you do also.

2

God's Word is life, healing, and health to all who find it

*My son, attend to my words; consent and submit
to my sayings. Let them not depart from your sight;
keep them in the center of your heart.
For they are life to those who find them,
healing and health to all their flesh.*

Proverbs 4:20–22 AMPC

We all need healing at various times and in different ways. We may need spiritual healing, physical healing, emotional healing, or mental healing. We may need financial healing or healing in relationships. Jesus is our Healer, and He can heal you anywhere you hurt.

God works through various ways and means. He may heal you supernaturally through a miraculous healing, or He may work through a doctor, a counselor, a minister, or a friend to give you the help you need. Whether it happens through a miracle or through medication, surgery, physical therapy, or counseling, we should always remember that however healing comes, it is from Jesus.

When we feel we need healing, we should always ask Jesus for it and trust Him to work through any means He chooses. People who are physically sick or in pain need physical healing, and unless Jesus chooses to heal them miraculously, they will probably need to go to a doctor, who has the knowledge and skill to treat them effectively and who may prescribe medicine for them. People who are perpetually anxious and worried need mental healing. Perhaps they suffer from a mental condition such as depression, bipolar disorder, or schizophrenia. I have heard many testimonies from people who were completely healed of mental illnesses through studying and meditating on God's Word. I have also heard of others who have been healed through counseling and some type of medication.

Sometimes healing comes quickly, and sometimes it is a long process, but we know that God is our Healer, and He heals in His ways and in His timing. We don't get to choose how or when God heals us, but we know that He will, because this is what His Word tells us.

If people have been emotionally wounded through abuse, rejection, criticism, or other experiences, they need emotional healing. Isaiah 61:3 says that God will give us beauty for ashes, meaning that He will redeem the negative experiences that could destroy us and bring beauty and strength out of our pain.

Because of the sexual abuse I suffered during my childhood, I desperately needed emotional healing, but I had no idea that Jesus would provide healing for me because I had never been told that He would. I needed emotional stability because my emotions were wounded, and I lived according to my feelings, which were fickle and unreliable. Years ago, when I read about healing in the Bible, I assumed it referred only to spiritual healing, such as God's gift of eternal life through Jesus, but I was wrong. Thankfully, I discovered in Psalm 147:3 that Jesus heals us when we are brokenhearted, and He binds up our wounds.

I also needed mental healing because my thoughts were not in agreement with God's Word. My mind needed to be renewed (Romans 12:2; 2 Corinthians 10:4–5), and God's Word does this. If you learn God's Word, you will be able to discern when a thought comes to your mind that is not a godly one, and then you can reject it and replace it with God's thoughts. Our thoughts guide our life. They are the basis for our decisions, and if they are wrong, then our lives will go in the wrong direction.

God cares about everything
that concerns you.

God cares about everything that concerns us, and He has compassion for us and delights in showing us His power and mercy. But He wants us to ask for His help. The apostle James writes: "You do not have because you do not ask God" (James 4:2), and Jesus says whatever we ask in His name, He will do (John 14:13). I encourage you to begin asking for more than you have ever asked for before, because you cannot ask God for too much. He "is able to do immeasurably more than all we ask or imagine" (Ephesians 3:20).

Many people mistakenly believe that Jesus came to earth only to forgive sins and make a way for us to go to heaven when we die, but He came for much more than that. He came that we might have and enjoy a good life while we are here on earth (John 10:10). I went to church for many years before I learned that I could go to Jesus when I needed healing of any kind and trust Him to provide it. If that is also your story, I encourage you to go to Jesus anytime you need healing. Ask Him either to give you a miracle or to guide you in what you should do or where you can seek help.

God's Word is like medicine for our souls; it "is

alive and full of power [making it active, operative, energizing, and effective]" (Hebrews 4:12 AMPC). When you need healing of any kind, I urge you to try God's Word and let it act as medicine for your soul. It is free, and you can have all the refills you want.

God's Word is medicine for your soul.

3

❧

God's Word
heals and delivers

❧

*He sends forth His word and heals them
and rescues them from the pit and destruction.*

Psalm 107:20 AMPC

Our enemy, the devil (Satan), is dedicated to the destruction of God's children and His plan for their lives. Satan was once a beautiful archangel, but because he rebelled against God and said he would raise his throne above God's, he and the angels who rebelled with him were thrown out of heaven and cast down to the earth (Isaiah 14:12–15). This occurred before God created the earth as we know it and before He created the first human beings, Adam and Eve.

Genesis 3:1–6 tells us that Satan approached Eve in the form of a serpent and deceived her through lies. He convinced her to do what God had specifically told her not to do, and she convinced Adam to do the same. From that time on, humanity has suffered in various ways, but God did not leave people helpless. He had a plan from the very beginning—a plan that His Son, Jesus, would come to earth to rescue and deliver all humankind from the destruction the devil had planned.

In order to have God's help, all any person has to do is believe in Jesus. This means to believe that He died for our sins and was raised from the dead, and that every promise in God's Word is true and available to all those who will believe.

Have you ever felt as though you have fallen into a pit of despair, depression, or discouragement, and you don't know how to get out? I have, and I am glad to know that when I cannot help myself, God's Word is available to help me. Jesus is the Word made flesh (John 1:14), and when the Word helps us, Jesus helps us.

If we are discouraged or in despair or if we feel depressed, we can go to the Psalms and read how David, who wrote many of the Psalms, often felt the same way. But the Psalms also show us how David trusted God to lift him out of the pit and deliver him from the destruction his enemies had planned for him (Psalm 40).

Satan wants to destroy your body, mind, emotions, relationships, finances, joy, peace, and anything else God wants you to enjoy. He works tirelessly and continuously to destroy us, but the good news is that Jesus has already provided all we need for healing and help in any area of our life. All we need to do is claim it as ours and remind ourselves that the devil is a liar.

Satan often works through unsuspecting people to bring pain into our lives. He used my parents to begin what he intended to be a cycle of destruction in my life, but I cried out to God, and He rescued me. He didn't get me out of the situation I was in as a child, but He gave me the strength and grace to go through it, and now He uses me to lead others out of their own destructive cycles.

Satan is a deceiver, and he wants us to think that people are our problem or even that God is causing our problems. But we must look past whoever or whatever Satan is using and see that he is the real enemy. The good news is that we have power and authority over him (Luke 10:19). If we submit ourselves to God, we can resist the devil and he will flee (James 4:7).

In order to resist the enemy, we must recognize when he is at work and resist him at the onset of his attack. First Peter 5:8 tells us to be vigilant because our adversary the devil "roams around like a lion roaring [in fierce hunger], seeking someone to seize upon and devour" (AMPC). You and I don't have to be devoured if we know God's Word. God's Word will deliver us. God's Word will heal us.

4

God's Word
protects us

*As for God, His way is perfect! The word of the Lord
is tested and tried; He is a shield to all those
who take refuge and put their trust in Him.*

Psalm 18:30 AMPC

A shield protects us, and God is a shield to all who put their trust in Him. This doesn't mean that Satan cannot attack us, but it does mean that he cannot do us any permanent harm. Jesus says that in the world we will have "tribulation and trials and distress and frustration; but be of good cheer [take courage; be confident, certain, undaunted]! For I have overcome the world" (John 16:33 AMPC).

Satan is the ruler of this world's systems, but if we function according to God's system (His Word), then no matter what Satan tries to do, we will win in the end. Paul writes in Romans 8:28 that all things work together for good to those who love God and want His will (what He desires). Joseph is a good example of this. In Genesis, we read about how his brothers treated him cruelly, but he told them that what they intended for harm, God intended for good (Genesis 50:20). Joseph's brothers had been jealous and envious of him and sold him into slavery, but God was with him (Acts 7:9).

It doesn't matter who is against us because God is with us, and He is greater than any enemy. God lives in us, as believers in Jesus Christ, and the Bible says that He who is in us is greater than he who is in the world (1 John 4:4).

It doesn't matter who is against you
because God is with you.

Multiple times in the Bible, God tells us that we don't have to be afraid because He is with us (Joshua 1:9; Matthew 1:23; 28:20; Hebrews 13:5). We don't even have to know how He plans to help us; all we need to know is that He loves us and is with us. He says in Isaiah 41:10:

> So do not fear, for I am with you; do not be dismayed, for I am your God. I will strengthen you and help you; I will uphold you with my righteous right hand.

Satan fears the name of Jesus, the blood of Jesus, and the Word of God. These three are mighty weapons, and we should depend on them as we put our faith in God. When the enemy tries to defeat you, pray in Jesus' name or simply say, "Satan, I come against you in Jesus' name." Remind Satan of the blood of

Jesus that was shed for you and speak God's Word. These are your best defenses against the devil.

The Holy Spirit led Jesus into the wilderness to be tested and tempted by the devil for forty days and nights. Each time the devil lied to Him, Jesus said, "It is written" and quoted Scripture that refuted the devil's lie (Matthew 4:1–10). Speak God's Word and then trust Him while you wait on Him for deliverance. Keep helping other people. While you are waiting for your breakthrough, you can help and bless others by doing good and making their lives better.

God's thoughts and ways are perfect; they are higher than our thoughts and ways (Isaiah 55:8–9). People make plans in their minds, but God directs their steps (Proverbs 16:9). We need to pray for God's wisdom and direction, because Proverbs 16:25 says that when we try to manage our life on our own, there is a way that seems right to us, but at the end of it is death and destruction. Often, God's ways don't make sense to us, but that is because we are looking at them with our carnal (fleshly) mind. For example, God's Word tells us that if we need more, we should give away some of what we have (Luke 6:38). How can we have more if we give away what we have? The answer is "Because God said so." If we will do what God's Word teaches us to do whether we understand it or not, we will see great things happen in our lives (Galatians 6:7–9).

Even though my parents had abused me throughout my childhood, God led me to take care of them when they were older and to provide for them as I would want to be provided for until they died (Exodus 20:12). This was one of the most challenging things I have ever done. But with God's help, I did it. It took effort, time, and lots of money, but I have seen God reward my obedience in my life. If you obey God, you too will see His reward in your life, and your joy and peace will abound, because the more difficult the obedience, the greater the reward.

The more difficult the obedience,
the greater the reward.

5

_❧_

Meditating on God's Word brings wisdom, prosperity, and success

_❧_

*This Book of the Law shall not depart out of
your mouth, but you shall meditate on it day
and night, that you may observe and do according
to all that is written in it. For then you shall
make your way prosperous, and then you shall
deal wisely and have good success.*

Joshua 1:8 AMPC

Wisdom is the correct use of knowledge, and it is one of the most valuable assets we can have. What good is knowledge if we don't know how to apply it wisely? I say, "Wisdom is doing now what you will be satisfied with later." We may not always *feel* like doing the wise thing, but if we do it anyway, we will eventually be glad we did.

Wisdom is doing now what you will be satisfied with later.

Hebrews 12:11 says that no discipline seems joyous when we are going through it, but later on "it yields a peaceable fruit of righteousness to those who have been trained by it" (AMPC). Do you care about later on? Many people live only for the moment without thinking seriously about the future and how their current actions will affect it. This kind of thinking is unwise because "later on" always comes and brings the results of decisions we have made in the past. Once we have those results, it is too late to go back and undo what we have done. Of course, God will forgive our foolish-ness, but we may still have to deal with the results of it.

PROSPERITY

We all want to prosper in our labors, and God prom-ises prosperity to those who meditate on His Word. To *meditate* means to roll over and over in the mind and to mutter softly. I tell people that if they know how to worry, they know how to meditate. When we worry, we meditate on our problems, but when we meditate on God's Word, we meditate on the answers to our problems.

---

*When you meditate on God's Word,
you meditate on the answers
to your problems.*

The Word *prosperity* means wholeness. It means to flourish, to bloom, to triumph, to grow, or to have suf-ficiency of means. If we understand this, who would not want true prosperity? We all do, and meditating on God's Word will release it into our lives. When we meditate on God's Word, we begin to see the wisdom of obeying it. When we see the wisdom of obedience and act on it, then we will succeed in all we put our hand to. It's vitally important for us to realize that knowing God's Word is not what causes us to be a success; *doing it* does. However, we cannot obey the Word unless we know it, and meditating on it helps us to know it—not only mentally, but in a deeper way. Meditating on the Word helps us know it so deeply that it becomes part of our lives. When God's Word becomes part of who we are, then all of our choices are made in agreement with it.

Some people think prosperity refers only to money, but it encompasses so much more than that. A person may have a lot of money and still not have what it takes to make a life successful. We have no real success unless we have peace, joy, a good relationship with God, friends, and fruitfulness that cause us to know that our life has not been wasted. We are not prosperous unless we are content. I don't mean that we are content to the point that we never want change, but content with where we are in the present moment because we believe we are in God's hands and that His ways and timing are perfect in our lives.

SUCCESS

What does it take for a person to be successful? Is it reaching the top of the corporate ladder? Some people do reach the top of a so-called ladder and then find their ladder is leaning against the wrong building. Some people think success is having a lot of money, but when a person is on their deathbed, they will not ask for their checkbook balance. They will want God, family, and friends.

I believe that success is knowing God and having an intimate relationship with Him. I also believe that success is knowing yourself—your strengths and your weaknesses—and embracing the unique person that God created you to be.

---

*Success is knowing God and having
an intimate relationship with Him.*

6

God's Word brings stability, fruitfulness, and prosperity

And he shall be like a tree firmly planted [and tended] by the streams of water, ready to bring forth its fruit in its season; its leaf also shall not fade or wither; and everything he does shall prosper [and come to maturity].

Psalm 1:3 AMPC

To understand Psalm 1:3, we need to know Psalm 1:2, where the psalmist writes about someone who is blessed, saying: "But his delight and desire are in the law of the Lord, and on His law (the precepts, the instructions, the teachings of God) he habitually meditates (ponders and studies) by day and by night" (AMPC). A person who desires, delights in, meditates on, and studies God's Word is characterized by stability, fruitfulness, and prosperity.

STABILITY

A tree firmly planted will not be affected by the storms of nature. Dave and I have a huge, old, deeply rooted oak tree in our backyard, and although we have endured many storms in the years we have lived here, that tree has not sustained any damage other than a few broken branches. Other trees have been destroyed, uprooted, and blown away by the storms, but not the firmly planted oak tree.

Isaiah 61:3 says that those of us who belong to God will become "trees of righteousness, the planting of the Lord, that He may be glorified" (NKJV). God wants us to be firmly planted in His Word and not to be affected by the storms of life. Not all storms are in the forecast, meaning we cannot foresee all the difficult situations we may encounter in life. We all face unexpected circumstances that are unpleasant, and the way we handle those things reveals a lot about our character and maturity.

God wants you to be firmly planted in His Word.

We make a big mistake if we think every day will be just as we plan it to be. A few weeks ago, I was having a peaceful day, and suddenly someone heard something that made them angry. I ended up in the path of the anger and got drawn into the situation without wanting to be. It took about two days of my life to get that particular storm calmed, and it wasn't even my storm! The situation was frustrating, and I was tempted to stay angry with the person who didn't control their temper, but then God reminded me that I teach others to forgive quickly and I needed to do the same. (Ouch! I don't like it when God preaches my own sermons to me.)

I immediately started praying, asking God to help me obey Him and forgive swiftly. Because my emotions were stirred up, I knew I needed God's help. He did help me, and I was able to forgive, let go of the situation, and move on with my life as if nothing had happened.

How do you handle the storms of life? Do you do what God's Word says to do, regardless of how you feel? Or do you become emotional and unstable? God is always available to help you handle life's storms in a godly way. All you need to do is ask.

FRUITFULNESS

Meditating on God's Word brings fruitfulness, and that is an important thing. Today, people are very busy, but that doesn't mean they are busy doing what will bear good fruit for God (meaning to make a positive difference in the world and to bring honor to Him, or to be productive) in their life. God has not called us to be busy, but He has called us to be fruitful.

God has called you to be fruitful, not busy.

Jesus says that if we abide in Him, we will bear "much fruit" (John 15:5 NKJV). To *abide* means to live, dwell, and remain in. Meditating on God's Word is part of the abiding lifestyle. We cannot have only a forty-five-minute visit with Jesus on Sunday morning during a church service and not think of Him until the next Sunday, yet expect to live a fruitful life. Abiding in Christ in our lifestyle means we include Him in everything we do and acknowledge Him in all things. We talk to Him, think about Him, and think about His Word throughout each day.

It also means that God's Word rules, and when a decision needs to be made, we make the one that agrees with His Word. There are two words that can never go together in the life of a Christian: "No, Lord!"

If He is our Lord, then our answer must always be yes. It can never be no.

PROSPERITY

It is important for us to remember that the word *prosperity* refers to more than financial abundance. It is a word that describes wholeness and conveys a sense of thriving in every area of our lives. Certainly, people can prosper financially, but we can also prosper in our relationships, in the way we enjoy and use the gifts and talents God has given us, and in life's intangible qualities, such as love, joy, peace, and a sense of purpose.

Abiding in God and His Word brings stability, fruitfulness, and prosperity into our lives. When people see these blessings in our lives, our witness for Christ is strengthened, because people see the goodness of God and desire to have the life He offers.

7

❧

God's Word upholds, guides, maintains, and propels the universe

❧

He is the sole expression of the glory of God
[the Light-being, the out-raying or radiance of
the divine], and He is the perfect imprint and very
image of [God's] nature, upholding and maintaining
and guiding and propelling the universe by
His mighty word of power. When He had by offering
Himself accomplished our cleansing of sins
and riddance of guilt, He sat down at
the right hand of the divine Majesty on high.

Hebrews 1:3 AMPC

When we ponder the universe and how marvelous it is, we might wonder what keeps Earth spinning perfectly on its axis or how the sun, moon, and stars stay in the sky without falling. I love to watch nature programs because they remind me of how amazing God is and how much beyond our understanding His creation is.

To know what God is like, study Jesus.

Jesus is the perfect image and imprint of God's nature. If you want to know what God is like, study Jesus. Hebrews 1:3 states that God not only upholds but maintains the universe. I wonder how much maintenance the universe requires to keep it running perfectly?

The galaxy in which you and I live is the Milky Way, but there are at least two trillion other galaxies, and more are being discovered every day. Estimates range from 100 billion to 400 billion stars in the Milky Way alone, and I seriously wonder who counted them. I doubt that anyone accurately knows what all is in the universe that God is holding together every moment that we live. Think of the disaster that would take place if God withheld His maintenance for even one second.

He keeps this world functioning correctly and upholds "all things by the word of His power" (Hebrews 1:3 NKJV). His Word has *that* much power, so surely it can keep us maintained, upheld, and guided. Put your trust in God! He alone is completely reliable. God loves you and desires to take care of you even as He cares for the rest of His creation, and He will if you let Him.

I suggest you take some time to deeply think about what it means when the Bible says that Jesus upholds, maintains, and propels the universe by the word of His power. If you do, it will give you a glimpse of how powerful His Word is and will help you to put your trust in it.

GUIDANCE

Jesus guides the universe. He keeps it going in the right direction every second of every day. Not only that, but He desires to guide our lives in the same way. He has given us the Holy Spirit as our guide in life (John 14:15–17, 26). He lives inside of us and is always trying to guide us in the right direction and help us make the right decisions. He teaches us the truth of God's Word, and when we believe this, we will know the direction we should take in every situation. I encourage you to trust God, relax, rest in Him, and enjoy the life He has given you. Don't waste it being anxious, worried, fearful, jealous, envious, unforgiving, or negative—that will steal what Jesus died to give you. Decide today that if Jesus can guide and maintain the universe, then surely He can do the same thing for you.

8

God's Word has the power to create

In the beginning God created the heavens and the earth. Now the earth was formless and empty, darkness was over the surface of the deep, and the Spirit of God was hovering over the waters. And God said, "Let there be light," and there was light. God saw that the light was good, and he separated the light from the darkness. God called the light "day," and the darkness he called "night." And there was evening, and there was morning—the first day.

Genesis 1:1–5

The first chapter of Genesis, which is the first chapter of the Bible, is the story of creation. Notice in the Scripture passage above that God said, "Let there be light," and light was made (Genesis 1:3). This happened on the first day of creation.

On the second day:

> God said, "Let there be a vault between the waters to separate water from water." So God made the vault and separated the water under the vault from the water above it. And it was so. God called the vault "sky." And there was evening, and there was morning—the second day.
>
> Genesis 1:6–8

The following day, God spoke again, saying:

> "Let the water under the sky be gathered to one place, and let dry ground appear." And it was so. God called the dry ground "land," and the gathered waters he called "seas." And God saw that it was good. Then God said, "Let the land produce vegetation: seed-bearing plants and

trees on the land that bear fruit with seed in it, according to their various kinds." And it was so. The land produced vegetation: plants bearing seed according to their kinds and trees bearing fruit with seed in it according to their kinds. And God saw that it was good. And there was evening, and there was morning—the third day.

Genesis 1:9–13

Are you beginning to see a pattern? Every time God created something, He did it by speaking. God said something, and whatever He said came into existence. Let's look at what happened on the fourth day:

And God said, "Let there be lights in the vault of the sky to separate the day from the night, and let them serve as signs to mark sacred times, and days and years, and let them be lights in the vault of the sky to give light on the earth." And it was so. God made two great lights—the greater light to govern the day and the lesser light to govern the night. He also made the stars. God set them in the vault of the sky to give light on the earth, to govern the day and the night, and to separate light from darkness. And God saw that it was good. And there was evening, and there was morning—the fourth day.

Genesis 1:14–19

On the fifth day:

God said, "Let the water teem with living creatures, and let birds fly above the earth across the vault of the sky." So God created the great creatures of the sea and every living thing with which the water teems and that moves about in it, according to their kinds, and every winged bird according to its kind. And God saw that it was good. God blessed them and said, "Be fruitful and increase in number and fill the water in the seas, and let the birds increase on the earth." And there was evening, and there was morning—the fifth day.

Genesis 1:20–23

On the sixth day of creation, a *lot* happened:

And God said, "Let the land produce living creatures according to their kinds: the livestock, the
creatures that move along the ground, and the
wild animals, each according to its kind." And
it was so. God made the wild animals according
to their kinds, the livestock according to their
kinds, and all the creatures that move along the
ground according to their kinds. And God saw
that it was good. Then God said, "Let us make
mankind in our image, in our likeness, so that
they may rule over the fish in the sea and the
birds in the sky, over the livestock and all the
wild animals, and over all the creatures that
move along the ground." So God created mankind in his own image, in the image of God he
created them; male and female he created them.
God blessed them and said to them, "Be fruitful and increase in number; fill the earth and
subdue it. Rule over the fish in the sea and the
birds in the sky and over every living creature
that moves on the ground." Then God said, "I
give you every seed-bearing plant on the face
of the whole earth and every tree that has fruit

with seed in it. They will be yours for food. And to all the beasts of the earth and all the birds in the sky and all the creatures that move along the ground—everything that has the breath of life in it—I give every green plant for food." And it was so. God saw all that he had made, and it was very good. And there was evening, and there was morning—the sixth day.

Genesis 1:24–31

Notice again that every time God spoke, something came into existence.

You and I have the privilege of speaking God's Word today and seeing good things created in and through our lives. When we speak His Word, we are simply agreeing with Him.

When you speak God's Word,
you are agreeing with Him.

In Psalm 2:7, the psalmist writes of the coming Messiah: "*I will declare the decree:* The Lord has said to Me, 'You are My Son, today I have begotten You' " (NKJV, italics mine). To *declare the decree* means to speak forth the things that are written. As we speak the Word that is written for our instruction—God's Word—we see its creative power in our lives.

9

಄

God's Word brings blessing to those who order their conduct and conversation according to it

ೃ

Blessed (happy, fortunate, to be envied) are the undefiled (the upright, truly sincere, and blameless) in the way [of the revealed will of God], who walk (order their conduct and conversation) in the law of the Lord (the whole of God's revealed will).

Psalm 119:1 AMPC

Knowing God's Word must be first on our list of priorities, but knowing it is not enough. Knowledge brings responsibility, and to know what is right to do and not do it is sin (James 4:17). God's Word teaches us what to do, and once we know what to do, it is our job with God's help to order or choose our behavior and conversation according to the revealed will of God we now know. Overcoming our problems requires us to speak according to God's Word, not according to our circumstances.

Speak according to God's Word,
not your circumstances.

This becomes a lifelong challenge for all of us. We want to do right, but in moments of weakness, we make wrong choices. When we have made an unwise choice, we then repent, and God forgives us. We receive His forgiveness and press toward the goal once more.

CONDUCT

Our conduct is important because it is what people see and judge. A woman once worked on our staff, and she was late for work more often than she was on time. I spoke to her several times about her tardiness, and she always told me her heart was right, and I believe it was. She wanted to be on time for work, but she was not ordering (disciplining) her conduct in ways that helped her get to work on time. She got caught up doing things at home or talking on the phone at home when she should have been driving to work. I finally told her plainly, "Your heart may be right, but if you continue to be late for work, I will have to let you go." After that, she was rarely late for work.

According to 1 Samuel 16:7, God looks at the heart, and having a good heart certainly sets us up for good behavior. God sees the heart, but people see our conduct, so I encourage you to realize that no matter how right your heart is, your conduct is what people notice and that becomes your witness about Jesus.

God sees your heart,
but people see your conduct.

CONVERSATION

The Amplified Bible, Classic Edition offers particular insight into the truth that we are to order our conversation according to God's Word. I think this is because what we say is very important. Our words come from our heart, and they help guide our actions. Thinking and saying the right things are the forerunners to doing the right things.

If I say I cannot do something, I probably won't do it. But if I say I can do something, then actually doing it becomes more likely. The apostle Paul writes, "I can do all things through Christ who strengthens me" (Philippians 4:13 NKJV). Paul believed and spoke that he could do whatever he needed to do with God's help. The more we say something, the more we believe it ourselves, because we hear and feed on our own words.

This is why negative people rarely, if ever, accomplish anything positive. They don't overcome obstacles because they don't believe they can. God is positive. He always believes in us, whether we believe in ourselves or not. Even though He believes in us, unless we agree with Him, we will not see the result we wish to see.

God believes in you, whether or not
you believe in yourself.

Before I learned the importance of my words, I made many negative comments about myself, which did not agree with God's Word. When I became angry with myself because of failures or mistakes I had made, or because other people had said negative things about me, I became totally emotional and spoke based on those emotions. I said things like "I'm so stupid; I never do anything right," or "Everything is always my fault" or "There's no point in even trying because I will fail anyway." Can you relate? Do you also speak negatively about yourself at times?

Search God's Word to see what it says about you, and then order your conversation in agreement with it. Do this even if you don't fully believe it yet. Declare God's Word until you believe it, then speak it in faith and watch it come to pass.

When you believe God's Word,
you can speak it in faith
and watch it come to pass.

When your conduct and your conversation agree with God's Word, great things can happen in your life.

10

※

God's Word cleanses
and purifies

※

*You are already clean because
of the word I have spoken to you.*

John 15:3

When I read that Jesus told His disciples that they were clean because of the word He had spoken to them, I wondered how this statement could be accurate. After all, three times Peter denied even knowing Christ (Matthew 26:69–75), Thomas struggled with doubt (John 20:24–25), and the disciples argued over which of them was the greatest (Luke 9:46–48), so I don't see how they could be called "clean." But then I read something that gave me a great answer: "Weakness is different than wickedness." I love that. The disciples had weaknesses, as we all do, but they were not wicked. They heard and received God's Word, and it did a work in them.

In Psalm 119:9, the psalmist asks God: "How can a young person stay on the path of purity? By living according to your word." This is true not only for young people, but for all of us. God's Word changes and purifies our heart, and God looks at the heart (1 Samuel 16:7). You might say that the Word gives us a new "want to." Once we receive Jesus and begin to study His Word, we don't want to sin. We want to do things the way He wants us to do them. But we do make mistakes, and as the apostle Paul writes, we must let go of what lies behind and press toward the things that are ahead (Philippians 3:12–14).

As we continue to study God's Word and spend time with Him, we are transformed into the Lord's image with ever-increasing glory (2 Corinthians 3:18). The Word does change us. Hebrews 4:12 says: "For the word of God is alive and active. Sharper than any double-edged sword, it penetrates even to dividing soul and spirit, joints and marrow; it judges the thoughts and attitudes of the heart." God's Word has inherent power to change us.

Instead of struggling to try to change ourselves, we should study what God's Word says about our weaknesses and trust that God will give us the grace and strength to do His will. For example, if you have an anger issue, then study everything the Bible says about anger, and it will be like taking medicine for the anger problem in your soul. It's the same principle as taking the right physical medicine for physical sickness. If a person has a headache, they take a pain reliever. They don't put a bandage on their head, thinking it will cure their headache. Likewise, if we cut our arm, we don't put an aspirin in the wound; we bandage it. We should learn how to apply God's Word in the same way.

Study what God's Word says about the areas of your life you want to improve, and little by little, Jesus will change you, because He is the Word (John 1:1). The more time you spend studying and meditating on God's Word, and the more time you spend with Him in prayer developing your relationship with Him, the more you will be changed into His image. Total transformation usually doesn't happen overnight; what's important is that you make a little more progress each day. And remember to celebrate your victories instead of feeling guilty about your weaknesses, trusting that because your heart is right, your behavior will improve.

11

God's Word reduces our capacity to sin and strengthens us against temptation

I have hidden your word in my heart
that I might not sin against you.

Psalm 119:11

I have learned that when I am tempted to sin, the best thing I can do is turn to God's Word. I may know specific verses that will help me deal with certain situations, or I may need to search for them in a concordance (a book that lists Bible references according to key words) or on the internet. Once I find those scriptures, I read them, meditate on them, and declare them aloud—and they help me overcome the temptation. For example, if I am worried about something, I know that anxiety is not God's will for me, and I depend on Philippians 4:6–7: "Do not be anxious about anything, but in every situation, by prayer and petition, with thanksgiving, present your requests to God. And the peace of God, which transcends all understanding, will guard your hearts and your minds in Christ Jesus."

I wrote an entire book called *The Answer to Anxiety* based on Philippians 4:6–7 because I believe this passage is the answer to anxiety. However, I also rely on other scriptures, such as Matthew 6:25–34, when I am tempted to worry. God often reminds me to take life one day at a time, and Matthew 6:34 encourages me to do this, saying: "Therefore do not worry about tomorrow, for tomorrow will worry about itself. Each day has enough trouble of its own."

If I struggle to forgive someone who has hurt or offended me, I know where to go in God's Word to be strengthened against the temptation to stay angry with that person. God's Word is not only for a Sunday morning church service; it should be interwoven into our daily lives. It is the spiritual food we need to live a godly life. I strongly encourage you to ponder the power of God's Word and let it help you in your everyday life.

I cannot encourage you strongly enough to rely on God's Word. Depend on it and believe that meditating on it is like chewing the food you eat. When you chew your food, the nutrients in it are released to keep you healthy. If you swallow it whole, you won't get its full benefits. Meditate (chew) on God's Word so it can keep you spiritually healthy and strong.

Satan constantly tries to deceive us and draw us into sin. For this reason, we need to resist him immediately. Remember, when he tempted Jesus in the wilderness, Jesus responded with Scripture, saying, "It is written" and then quoted God's Word (Matthew 4:4,

7, 10). We should follow the example Jesus set for us, speaking God's Word to the enemy when he tempts us. We can defeat his lies as we believe and declare what God's Word says.

David said he had hidden God's Word in his heart so he would not sin against Him (Psalm 119:11). When we regularly and diligently study God's Word, we hide it in our hearts, and it comes to the surface when we need it. Then we don't have to look up scriptures when we need them, because they are in our heart. One of the ministries of the Holy Spirit is to remind us of what we need to know when we need it (John 14:26), and He equips us with God's Word when we battle temptation. If you are a student of God's Word, you have scriptures hidden in your heart. You may not realize they are there, but when you need them, they will come to your mind. Helping us to recall His Word is one of the major ways God speaks to us.

God speaks to you by helping you recall His Word.

Many people think they don't hear from God, but the number one way He speaks is through His Word. If you don't study God's Word, you are not likely to hear from Him when you need to hear something, but if you do study it, I can promise you that it will be there when you need it.

12

❧

God's Word renews and revives us

❧

I am greatly afflicted; renew and revive me [giving me life], O Lord, according to Your word.

Psalm 119:107 AMP

All of us feel weary at times, for a variety of reasons. We may have been working too hard without a break, we may have been sick for a long time, we may be caring for a loved one who is infirm, or perhaps we have endured some kind of loss. Whatever the challenge may be that is causing us to experience weariness, God's Word can renew and revive us.

I often lean on Matthew 11:28–30 when I feel weary. Jesus said:

> Come to me, all you who are weary and burdened, and I will give you rest. Take my yoke upon you and learn from me, for I am gentle and humble in heart, and you will find rest for your souls. For my yoke is easy and my burden is light.

God's Word always gives us hope that things will change and reminds us that God will give us the strength we need to deal with whatever we are going through until it ends.

At times, we simply grow tired of doing what we are doing. Even if we want to do it, we can still reach a point where we need to be renewed or refreshed. I love teaching God's Word and writing, but occasionally I become weary of all the work that goes into it. I wouldn't want to do anything else, but I reach a point where I need to be refreshed. I need to study God's Word for myself, not just to teach someone else. I study for myself daily, but I may need an extended period of time where I rest from my work and take time to build myself up spiritually.

When we grow weary, we should remember that pushing ourselves without taking time to let God renew and revive us is unwise. If we don't take breaks, we may become grouchy with other people or make emotional decisions that turn out bad for us.

The scriptures below let us know that God is the only being in the universe who never grows weary. Everyone else does at times, so when it happens to you, don't feel guilty. Instead, take time for the replenishment you need.

Do you not know? Have you not heard? The Lord is the everlasting God, the Creator of the ends of the earth. He will not grow tired or weary, and his understanding no one can fathom. He gives strength to the weary and increases the power of the weak. Even youths grow tired and weary, and young men stumble and fall; but those who hope in the Lord will renew their strength. They will soar on wings like eagles; they will run and not grow weary, they will walk and not be faint.

Isaiah 40:28–31

Taking a day simply to rest in the presence of the Lord and to wait on Him or hope in Him will renew your strength. Then you can go back to what you need to do with renewed zeal and passion and be able to enjoy it once again.

Everyone needs to do this. The CEO of a major corporation, a young mother with small children at home, and everyone in between needs to take time to rest and be refreshed. The world refers to this as R&R, rest and relaxation, and it is a well-known fact that those who do take time for R&R are more effective in the long run than those who grow weary and keep pushing because they think they must.

No matter how busy you are, you can find a way

to rest properly if you truly want to. If we don't do it by choice, we may end up being forced to do it due to physical sickness or mental and emotional burnout. Taking time from our usual activity and getting the rest we need is healthy for everyone. You deserve to be renewed, revived, and refreshed regularly, so don't deny yourself this important part of life.

13

❧

God's Word enables us to walk at liberty and at ease

❧

And I will walk at liberty and at ease,
for I have sought and inquired for
[and desperately required] Your precepts.

Psalm 119:45 AMPC

L ife can be difficult if we try to live according to the ways of the world, but when we know the ways of God, it changes everything. Life may not be easy, but we can learn to do hard things with ease when we trust God to give us the wisdom and strength for everything we need to do. The psalmist writes that he walks "at liberty and at ease" because he has sought and inquired for and desperately required God's precepts, meaning His teachings and His ways.

To walk at liberty means to enjoy freedom. Jesus says that if we continue in His Word, we will know the truth and the truth will make us free (John 8:31– 32). And Luke 4:18 says that Jesus came to set the captives free. One of the most negative emotions that holds people captive is fear, and having Jesus set us free from fear is very important. I grew up with fear as my constant companion. I was raised by abusive and dysfunctional parents and was constantly afraid my father would be angry with me or that I would be punished for something. Fear prevents liberty. But when we walk according to God's ways, we can live without fear of what will happen to us, because we know God loves us and will always take care of us.

We need not fear that God is angry with us. Although He can become angry at sin and injustice, He is not an angry God. He is merciful and kind, always ready to forgive those who admit their sin and repent.

Like the psalmist, we should desperately require and seek to know God's ways. This is the key to enjoying our lives and finding solutions to our problems. In addition to seeking to know God's ways, we should trust Him completely. When we believe (trust), we enter His rest, and that allows us to live with ease (Hebrews 4:3). We do not have to carry our burdens alone, because God is with us to help and guide us.

Are you doing things God's way or your own way? If you are trying to go your own way, you are probably frustrated, and life is hard. But you can repent (acknowledge your sin and ask God to forgive you), make a change, and go in the right direction right now. This is a core teaching of the gospel, and the gospel is good news. It always offers us a solution to our problems.

I recommend that you study God's Word not simply to absorb information, but with the commitment that you will do what you read. The apostle James says if we are hearers but not doers of the Word, we deceive ourselves by reasoning that is contrary to the truth (James 1:22 AMPC).

You may think, *Well, Joyce, I would be able to obey God more if I just didn't have so many pressures in life.* Jesus didn't come to remove all the pressures of life, but He did come to make you stronger. When you are stronger, the pressures that once defeated you won't bother you at all. You will be able to handle them with ease, because the Word causes us to walk at liberty and at ease. You are not alone, and you don't have to handle life's pressures by yourself. Jesus left the earth when His mission here was complete, but He didn't leave us alone; He sent His Holy Spirit to live in us and to help us (John 14:16–17). His Spirit is a holy helper who enables us to do anything God asks us to do.

Desperately require God's presence in your life, seek Him daily, and depend on Him in every situation. Then you will no longer experience a life that is so hard you don't think you can handle it. Remember, life will not always be easy, but we can live it with a holy ease if we put our faith in God.

14

God's Word is filled with promises of His mercy and grace

I entreated Your favor with my whole heart;
be merciful and gracious to me
according to Your promise.

Psalm 119:58 AMPC

God's Word contains thousands of promises. Among them we find promises of God's favor, mercy, and grace, along with many other blessings. If we understand favor, mercy, and grace, this is good news, but if we don't, then we might skim over these but fail to understand what amazing promises God offers us.

When we have favor with God and He gives us favor with people, it means He opens for us doors we could never open for ourselves. When you have God's favor, you may be chosen for a job over a hundred other applicants, people will like you and not even know why, and you will enjoy watching God do for you things that can only happen because He orchestrates them for you. Favor cannot be earned or deserved, but it can and should be received with gratitude. If you have not done so previously, I encourage you to begin praying for and expecting God's favor in your life.

Favor should be received with gratitude.

I have experienced God's favor many times. Store clerks have given me a sale price on an item when the sale ended the day before. I have held jobs I was not qualified for, based on my natural abilities or training, but God enabled me to do them. I have had opportunities to minister in areas outside the United States where no one had been allowed to minister the gospel previously. I am sure you have experienced similar things, but maybe you didn't realize they came from God's favor on your life.

In Psalm 119:58, the psalmist prays for God's favor. In this same prayer, he asks God to be merciful and gracious to him: "I entreated Your favor with my whole heart; be merciful and gracious to me according to Your promise" (AMPC).

Being merciful is part of God's character.

Mercy is absolutely amazing. Being merciful is part of God's character. Mercy is another blessing that cannot be earned or deserved. God gives it as an act of

His gracious nature and out of His great love for us, and this should inspire tremendous gratitude from us. In Psalm 23:6, David writes that God's goodness and mercy would follow him all the days of his life (NKJV). According to Lamentations 3:22–23, God's mercies are new every morning, and if it were not for God's mercies, we would be consumed (NKJV). We deserve punishment, but God gives us mercy. Can we do the same for others? This is what God wants us to do.

Because of Jesus, our high priest, who has been tempted as we have, yet without sinning, we can boldly approach God with our needs:

Let us then approach God's throne of grace with confidence, so that we may receive mercy and find grace to help us in our time of need.

Hebrews 4:16

Here is a wonderful scripture about God's mercy that always comforts me:

But because of his great love for us, God, who is rich in mercy, made us alive with Christ even

when we were dead in transgressions—it is by
grace you have been saved.

                                        Ephesians 2:4–5

Psalm 119:58 also reminds us that God is gracious. Grace is God's undeserved favor, and I like to
say it is also God's power coming to us freely to help
us do with ease what we could never do on our own
with any amount of struggle and effort. We are saved
by grace through faith (Ephesians 2:8), and we should
live the same way we are saved—by grace through
faith.

We need to ask God for His grace in everything we
do. With His help, things that would be impossible
for us to do are made possible. When we learn to ask
for and receive God's grace, life becomes easier and we
can live in God's rest and enjoy it in everything we do.

Life does not have to be a struggle when we live in
God's favor, mercy, and grace.

15

God's Word gives us good judgment, wise and right discernment, and knowledge

Teach me good judgment (discernment) and knowledge, for I have believed and trusted and relied on Your commandments.

Psalm 119:66 AMP

I believe we can summarize good judgment, right discernment, and knowledge with one word: *wisdom*. Wisdom is one of the most important qualities we can operate with, and it promises us long life, prosperity, safety, ease, fearlessness, success, and good health, among other blessings (Proverbs 1:33; 3:13–18; 4:6–7; Ecclesiastes 7:12; Matthew 7:24–29; Ephesians 1:16–21; 2 Chronicles 1:7–12).

In order to operate in wisdom, we must know God's Word and take our time making decisions, so that we know we are making wise ones. Wisdom stands at the intersections of life, calling out to us to follow her (Proverbs 1:20–21).

In addition to wisdom, it's also important for us to operate in discernment, which the Holy Spirit gives to us. Discernment helps us perceive the difference between good and evil, right and wrong, truth and error. I pray for discernment on a regular basis. Discernment is deeper than emotion or human thought, and if we seek it, we will make right decisions that lead us into a life we can enjoy.

We have all made decisions based on emotions and later regretted them. Some of those decisions may have been minor and may not have caused a great deal of trouble, but others may have been life altering. Let me encourage you to grow in wisdom by slowing down and taking time to really think about any important decisions you are making. Often it is best to sleep on a decision and see if you feel the same way the next morning as you did the night before. Another good exercise is to try to think about the consequences your decision will create in your life.

I love dogs, and more than once I have purchased a puppy based on emotions and then had to give it away because my lifestyle is too busy for me to do the work a puppy requires. I like the emotional and fun side of having one, but I don't really want the work. Everything we enjoy in life comes with responsibility, and we must consider both enjoyment and responsibility when making decisions.

Good judgment saves us a lot of trouble, anxiety, and stress. Most of us live fast, busy lives, and the only way to have good judgment, wise discernment, and knowledge is to slow down. The more quickly we make decisions, the more likely we are to make bad ones. Before you make your next decision, ask yourself if you are merely excited about it or if you truly have peace about it.

Wise people who use good judgment will prepare for the future by saving some of everything they make. They will also be generous in giving to those in need, and God promises many blessings to people who are generous to the poor. Both saving and giving are wise.

---

*Only a life guided by God's Word
can be truly enjoyed.*

In short, a life that is guided by God's Word is the only life we can truly enjoy. His Word has the answer to any problem we may face, and it shows us the right way and the wrong way to live. The choice is ours, but God advises us to choose what will minister life and bring blessings to others and ourselves.

16

꜊

God's Word is better than thousands of gold and silver pieces

꜊

The law from your mouth is more precious to me
than thousands of pieces of silver and gold.

Psalm 119:72

God's Word is full of scriptures warning us of the danger of the love of money. First Timothy 6:10 says: "For the love of money is a root of all evils; it is through this craving that some have been led astray and have wandered from the faith and pierced themselves through with many acute [mental] pangs" (AMPC).

When we put the pursuit of money and material goods ahead of God, we are making a huge mistake. The psalmist knew that knowing God's commands and following them were more important than all the money in the world. I am sure that he also knew that by following God's Word and putting Him first in his life all his financial needs would be met and he would live an abundant life.

If we seek first God's Kingdom, which according to the Amplified Bible, Classic Edition, is "His way of doing and being right," He promises to add to us all the other things we could want (Matthew 6:33). If we delight ourselves in God, He will give us the desires of our heart (Psalm 37:4).

Only God can give you true satisfaction.

Money alone can never satisfy us (Ecclesiastes 5:10). God created us for Himself, and only He can give us true satisfaction. Satan uses money and possessions to lure people away from relationship with God. He even tried to do this to Jesus when he tempted and tested Him during the forty days He was in the wilderness:

> The devil led him up to a high place and showed him in an instant all the kingdoms of the world. And he said to him, "I will give you all their authority and splendor; it has been given to me, and I can give it to anyone I want to. If you worship me, it will all be yours."
>
> Luke 4:5–7

Jesus immediately resisted the enemy's temptation by quoting Scripture, saying, "It is written: 'Worship the Lord your God and serve him only' " (Luke 4:8). If Satan tried to tempt even Jesus with the love of money, we can certainly expect to be tempted in the same way. We often hear stories about people who once loved God and then, when they were blessed with success, including money and possessions, they turned away from God and ended up losing everything.

As God led the Israelites through the wilderness toward the Promised Land, He told them He was taking them to a place where they would have an abundance of everything (Deuteronomy 8:7–9). Then He warned them not to think they had accumulated such wealth through their own efforts and told them not to forget Him. If they did forget Him, they would be destroyed (Deuteronomy 8:10–20).

There is nothing wrong with enjoying nice things and being financially blessed, but we have to be careful not to let our blessings pull us away from God. God's Word gives good direction to the wealthy:

> As for the rich in this present age, charge them not to be haughty, nor to set their hopes on the uncertainty of riches, but on God, who richly provides us with everything to enjoy. They are to do good, to be rich in good works, to be generous and ready to share, thus storing up treasure for themselves as a good foundation for

the future, so that they may take hold of that
which is truly life.

1 Timothy 6:17–19 ESV

Use possessions and money to serve God, be good
to people who are less fortunate than you, and always
keep God first in your life. Only then will you be qualified to properly handle success, wealth, and an abundance of material blessings.

17

❧

God's Word
makes us wiser than
our enemies

❧

Your commands are always with me
and make me wiser than my enemies.
Psalm 119:98

Being wiser than our enemies benefits us in many ways. It will keep us safe from anything they are plotting to do to harm or hurt us, and it helps us overcome their wicked plans. In Exodus 23:20, God sends an angel to lead His people into the place He has prepared for them. Speaking of this angel, He says to them: "If you listen carefully to what he says and do all that I say, I will be an enemy to your enemies and will oppose those who oppose you" (Exodus 23:22). This is a wonderful promise that helps eliminate fear and anxiety from our lives.

Like you, I have been hurt and endured many injustices in life, but I have also seen God deliver me and give me back double what my enemies took from me. Although my father abused me sexually for many years, God delivered me from the shame it caused and has given me honor.

God tells us to love our enemies, forgive them, pray for them, and bless them (Matthew 5:43–48; Luke 23:34). This is one way we are wiser than they are, because loving those who have hurt us enables us to overcome evil with good (Romans 12:21).

Loving our enemies is difficult to do because it

seems so unfair, but God will be our Vindicator if we do things His way. Just think of Jesus, who endured the pain and shame of the cross so that our sins might be forgiven. This wasn't fair as we think of fairness, but it was God's will. And after Jesus had obeyed His Father in heaven through His death on the cross, He was given "the name that is above every name, that at the name of Jesus every knee should bow, in heaven and on earth and under the earth" (Philippians 2:9–10).

After Jesus had obeyed His Father by dying on the cross so we could be saved, He ascended on high and sat down at the right hand of God to wait for His enemies to be made a footstool for His feet (Hebrews 10:12–13).

God always rewards obedience. The Bible actually says that in order to please God, we must believe that He exists and that "He is a rewarder of those who diligently seek Him" (Hebrews 11:6 NKJV). Do you believe that God is a rewarder? Do you believe that if you know, love, and obey His Word, He will make you wiser than your enemies? I pray you do.

Satan desires to attack and defeat God's children, but he cannot succeed if we give God's Word first place in our life. When we do, we gain wisdom and will recognize Satan's attacks instead of being deceived and defeated. It is God's will for us to always have victory, and the way we gain victory in every situation is by obeying His Word.

PRAY FOR YOUR ENEMIES

Jesus teaches us to love our enemies and pray for those who mistreat us (Matthew 5:44). When we pray for people, it gives God an open door to work in their lives. The choice to change is still up to them, but when we pray, we do what God asks us to do. Then we can release the problem to Him and enjoy our lives while we wait for Him to work. I prayed for my father to repent and receive Jesus as his Savior for more than thirty years. To my natural eyes, it looked as though he would never change. I had decided that praying for him was not doing any good, and I stopped for a while. But God told me not to give up and I contin-ued to pray. When my father was eighty years old, he did finally tell me he was sorry for the abuse, and he asked Dave and me to pray with him for salvation. I encourage you not to give up on praying for people. Your part is to pray; the results are up to God and the person you are praying for. Pray and release your enemies into God's hands, and you will have the joy of watching Him bring justice into your life.

Do not give up on praying for people.

18

God's Word gives us light and shows us how to live

Your word is a lamp to my feet
and a light to my path.

Psalm 119:105 AMPC

Psalm 119:105 is about God giving us guidance. His Word gives us direction and shows us what to do in every situation. Proverbs 3:5–7 also encourages us and lets us know that God will lead and guide us: "Trust in the Lord with all your heart and lean not on your own understanding; in all your ways submit to him, and he will make your paths straight. Do not be wise in your own eyes; fear the Lord and shun evil."

I like Proverbs 3:7, which warns us not to be wise in our own eyes. To me, this says I shouldn't even think I am wise enough to run and manage my own life without God's help.

The New King James Version translation of Proverbs 3:5–6 tells us that if we acknowledge God in all our ways, He will direct our paths. To acknowledge God simply means to tell Him that you want His will and are willing to change your planned direction as He leads you to do so. Acknowledging God shows Him respect. God often lets us do what we want to do, but sometimes a direction we intend to take will cause problems for us unless we have divine guidance from God. The Holy Spirit dwells inside of us, and one of

His jobs is to be our guide in life (1 Corinthians 3:16; John 14:16–17; 16:13).

When people climb a mountain that is new to them, they usually hire a guide who is experienced in climbing that particular mountain. When we have a guide, we don't waste our time making mistakes and going in the wrong direction. A guide can take you places you would have never thought of going, point out dangerous things you would not have noticed, and keep you out of trouble.

I am thankful to have had the Holy Spirit to guide me in my life and ministry. When I started in ministry, I had no experience and did not know what to do. But the Holy Spirit has led us step by step over the past forty years, and as long as we have followed His guidance, we have succeeded in the things we have done.

Isaiah shares this promise with us: "Whether you turn to the right or to the left, your ears will hear a voice behind you, saying, 'This is the way; walk in it'" (Isaiah 30:21). Of course, if we want to hear from God and be guided by Him, we have to listen to His voice and be willing to change if He shows us to do something other than we had planned.

Multiple scriptures tell us we need God's help in guiding our lives. For example:

- "In their hearts humans plan their course, but the Lord establishes their steps" (Proverbs 16:9).
- "There is a way that appears to be right, but in the end it leads to death" (Proverbs 14:12).
- Jesus says, "Apart from me you can do nothing" (John 15:5).

I cannot even imagine how awful my life would have turned out had I not had the Holy Spirit and God's Word guiding me. It is so easy to be led by our own thinking and emotions, but when we do this, we almost always get ourselves into trouble. I urge you to let the Word of God be a lamp to your feet and a light to your path. Follow the guidance of the Holy Spirit, and you will enjoy your life a lot more.

19

❧

God's Word accomplishes God's purpose

❧

*As the rain and the snow come down from heaven,
and do not return to it without watering the earth
and making it bud and flourish, so that it yields seed
for the sower and bread for the eater, so is my word
that goes out from my mouth: It will not return to
me empty, but will accomplish what I desire
and achieve the purpose for which I sent it.*

Isaiah 55:10–11

God's Word is so much more than a collection of ancient writings or a book of good advice; it is filled with inherent power. When God speaks, the power to accomplish what He says accompanies His words. He says in Isaiah 55:11 that His Word "will not return to me empty." The King James Version says it "shall not return unto me void." This means that it is not ineffective or powerless. When God speaks, things happen. This isn't because of the words themselves, it's because God—who is all-powerful—is the One who speaks them.

You release power by speaking God's Word.

Many times, we do not speak God's Word because we are so busy speaking our own words. We talk about how we feel, what we think, what we want to do, or who has hurt or offended us. These comments don't change our situations. But when we speak God's Word, we release power. His Word, spoken in faith from a believer's mouth, can change circumstances.

We deal with all sorts of facts in life, and we often think of facts as situations that simply are the way they are. We face facts in our relationships, our jobs, our finances, our health, and other areas of our lives. We don't think they can change. But when a fact meets God's Word, change is possible.

Think about this: In the New Testament, Jesus' friend Lazarus was dead (John 11:14). That was a fact. But when Jesus walked up to his tomb, where he had lain for four days, He simply spoke in a loud voice, "Lazarus, come out!" (John 11:43). And Lazarus walked out of the tomb (John 11:44).

There are many stories in the Gospels of times when Jesus spoke and facts changed. He raised the dead, healed the sick, brought liberty to the oppressed, restored sight to the blind, and caused the lame to walk—sometimes with just His words. We must never exalt the facts of our circumstances above the power of God's Word.

God's Word is filled with promises for anyone who will believe them and act according to them. You may be dealing with difficult facts in your life, and perhaps you are powerless to change them in your own strength. Let me encourage you to begin to speak God's Word in these circumstances. Realize that when you speak God's Word, believing and trusting God to perform it, it is powerful. And watch what God will do to change the situations for you.

I'm not saying that you should ignore the facts you are facing, but that you should adjust your perspective of them and realize that by the power of God's Word, they can change. His Word is truth (John 17:17), and truth is greater than facts.

In Luke 8:5–11, Jesus compares the Word of God to seed. Every natural seed has power in it—power to eventually become a tree, a flower, a vegetable, or whatever is within it. When you plant the seed of His Word in your heart by speaking it, praying it, believing it, and obeying it, it will produce a harvest and accomplish God's purpose in your life.

20

❧

God's Word
gives us hope

❧

You are my refuge and my shield;
I have put my hope in your word.

Psalm 119:114

Hope is an amazing thing. It is not an unstable quality that leads you to say, "Well, maybe God will do something about my situation, but I'm not sure." Biblical hope is not like the kind of hope people in the world talk about. Worldly hope is unstable and changes with our circumstances, but biblical hope is a confident expectation that something good is going to happen. *To hope* means to wait on God with expectation.

Proverbs 13:12 says that "hope deferred makes the heart sick, but a longing fulfilled is a tree of life." In other words, if we put off hoping for good things, we will become discouraged and depressed. Emotionally, we need the positive effects of hope in our life.

I am encouraged when I read that the God of hope fills me with joy and peace (Romans 15:13). I recall a time when I had lost my joy and was feeling down emotionally. After asking God what was wrong with me, He led me to this scripture, and I realized I had lost my joy and peace because I had a negative attitude about circumstances in my life instead of a hopeful expectation that God was going to do something wonderful for me.

Hebrews 6:19 teaches us that hope is the anchor of our souls. An anchor is what holds a ship in place when it is docked and waiting to sail once again. There are times when we may feel like our life is "docked." Nothing is happening and we are just waiting to see what God will do next. But true, biblical hope means we're waiting on God with confident expectation. So, when we wait with hope, it anchors our mind and emotions to God in faith.

Hope is the anchor of your soul.

God has a good plan for your life: " 'For I know the plans I have for you,' declares the Lord, 'plans to prosper you and not to harm you, plans to give you hope and a future' " (Jeremiah 29:11). Perhaps you have made a lot of mistakes and your life is a big mess right now. God has not forgotten or given up on His plan for you. Remember, His plan is to prosper you and to give you hope and a future. Thankfully, when we put our faith in God, we never have to look back; we can always look forward to the good things ahead. I've heard that if God wanted us to look behind us, He would have given us eyes in the back of our head.

I encourage you to voice your hope. When people ask about your troubles, tell them that your faith is in God and you have hope that He will do something wonderful.

The apostle Peter writes that we are born again into an "ever-living hope":

> Praised (honored, blessed) be the God and Father of our Lord Jesus Christ (the Messiah)! By His boundless mercy we have been born again to an ever-living hope through the resurrection of Jesus Christ from the dead.
>
> 1 Peter 1:3 AMPC

When we walk with God, we are never without hope, no matter what our circumstances may be or how long they have lasted. Let us give thanks for God's promise to help us when we are suffering. We are never alone or forgotten. Have hope and expect God to do something amazing in your life.

You are never alone or forgotten.

21

God's Word brings light and dispels darkness

The unfolding of your words gives light;
it gives understanding to the simple.

Psalm 119:130

Many people live in darkness, and I was one of them for a long time. Living in darkness means not knowing the truth of God's Word and living a life far below His will (what He desires for us). Darkness symbolizes all that is harmful, wicked, and evil. When we live in darkness, we are miserable, but we have no idea why. Only when the light comes into our life do we realize just how bad our life has been.

Jesus is the light of the world. He dispels darkness, and the darkness can never put out the light (John 1:5). He shows us and makes available to us the wonderful life that is ours if we want it.

When I was living in darkness, my behavior was totally selfish, I was angry, and I had no peace. I was filled with unforgiveness toward the people who had hurt me, and I had no joy. I really did not know there was any other way to live. The entrance of God's Word brings light to our lives (Psalm 119:130 NKJV), and as I began to study God's Word, I started seeing truth that would eventually set me free (John 8:32). I had to receive the truth and apply it to my life before I experienced change, and it was certainly not all easy, but it has been worth it. Now I live in the light.

God's Word teaches us what is right and what is wrong, and it shows us how to make godly choices that will release God's blessings into our lives. But we must apply God's Word and do what it says. James 1:22–25 teaches us that if we hear the Word but don't act in accordance with it, we deceive ourselves.

Many Christians mistakenly think their only spiritual responsibility is to go to church, but God also expects us to learn His Word and do what it says. When the world sees us walking in God's will and they observe the blessings this releases, they will want to know Jesus also. The best way for us to be witnesses for Christ is to do what we say we believe. Actions speak louder than words.

To be a witness for Christ,
do what you say you believe.

Jesus says that we are now the light of the world:

You are the light of the world. A town built on a hill cannot be hidden. Neither do people light a lamp and put it under a bowl. Instead they put it on its stand, and it gives light to everyone in the house. In the same way, let your light shine before others, that they may see your good deeds and glorify your Father in heaven.

Matthew 5:14–16

It is important for us to do the good works that God has prepared ahead of time for us to do (Ephesians 2:10). Our works don't get us into heaven, because we are saved by grace alone (Ephesians 2:8); however, our works do reveal the love and goodness of God to people in this world, and we receive rewards in heaven for what we have done during our earthly lifetime.

When God created the world, the Bible says that "darkness was on the face of the deep...Then God said, 'Let there be light'; and there was light" (Genesis 1:2–3 NKJV). Light was the first thing He created, which shows how important it is. Some people love darkness more than light because their deeds are evil (John 3:19–20). We should pray for those who dwell in darkness that they will let the light of God's Word into their lives so they may be delivered and set free.

22

❧

God's Word brings direction and shows us what to do

❧

Direct my footsteps according to your word;
let no sin rule over me.

Psalm 119:133

I truly believe that all the answers we need for any situation that arises can be found in God's Word. It instructs us in the way we need to live in order to enjoy the life that Jesus died for us to have. God's Word shows us what to do and what not to do, but we must choose to obey it. To know what is right to do and not do it is sin (James 4:17).

As the psalmist writes, when we let God's Word direct our footsteps, sin will not rule over us. We will still be tempted, but because we know the Word, we will recognize the temptation and resist it in the power of God.

Jesus says that if we love Him, we will obey Him (John 14:15). He already loves us perfectly and unconditionally. Our obedience doesn't make Him love us more, but it does show that we love Him.

When Peter and the other apostles were preaching in Jerusalem, the high priest told them not to preach in the name of Jesus (Acts 5:27–28), but they replied, "We must obey God rather than human beings!" (Acts 5:29). This is the attitude that we should all have, because if we are people-pleasers, we can end up disobeying God.

A people-pleaser can end up disobeying God.

Our obedience or disobedience not only affects our life, it affects everyone who is part of our life. Adam disobeyed God, and it caused many people to sin. But Jesus was obedient to God, and it made many people righteous (Romans 5:19).

Our children have often thanked Dave and me for being obedient to God, because they know our obedience has affected their lives in positive ways. Now, the choices they make are affecting their children (our grandchildren). We should remember that everything we do has a ripple effect.

Everything God tells us to do or not to do is for our benefit. If we believe this, being obedient will be easier even when it is hard to do. Possibly one of the most difficult commands to obey is to forgive, bless, and pray for our enemies (Luke 6:27–28; 23:34), but if we will do it, it releases many blessings into our lives. We should never base forgiveness on our feelings. Forgiveness is not a feeling, but a decision about how we treat the people who have hurt us. The goodness of God leads people to repentance (Romans 2:4), and when we are good to people who haven't been good to us, it can melt their hard hearts and help them be open to having a relationship with Jesus.

---

*Forgiveness is a decision about
how you treat people.*

I encourage you to spend time studying God's Word daily. We can never study it too much. Even reading the same Bible passages over and over is beneficial, because we tend to forget things and need to be reminded of them. In his letter to the Philippians, Paul told the people that it was "no trouble" for him to repeat the "same things" he had been teaching (Philippians 3:1). He knew they needed to hear God's Word over and over again. This is why the Bible includes so many scriptures about meditating on God's Word (Psalm 1:1–2; 119:15, 97). God told Joshua to meditate on the Word day and night, so he would observe and do according to all that is written in it and thereby make his way prosperous and have good success (Joshua 1:8 AMPC). The same instructions—and the same blessings—apply to you and me.

I have learned over the years to love God's Word. It keeps me in the light and directs my path. The time I spend in the Word is time well invested, and it will be for you also. Give the Word a primary place in your life, and when you need to know what to do, you will have the answers you need.

23

Jesus is the Word

*In the beginning was the Word, and the Word
was with God, and the Word was God. He was
with God in the beginning. Through him all things
were made; without him nothing was made that
has been made. In him was life, and that life
was the light of all mankind.*

John 1:1–4

It is important to remember that Jesus is the Word who became flesh and came to this earth to pay for our sins and save us (John 1:14; 1 Peter 2:24). Not only do we know this based on John 1:1–4, but we also read in Revelation 19:13, referring to Jesus: "He is dressed in a robe dipped in blood, and his name is the Word of God." Remembering that Jesus is the Word helps us reverence God's Word and realize that when we hear, read, or study Scripture, we are studying Jesus.

Jesus is God, and He reveals God the Father to us. He says, "Anyone who has seen me has seen the Father" (John 14:9). Studying the Word (Jesus) teaches us about the character of God. He is good, kind, merciful, loving, and forgiving. He also hates sin, but He does not hate sinners. He loves them and works with them to bring them to faith in Him. God is also holy, and we should have a reverential and respectful awe and fear of Him. I don't mean that we should be afraid of God in the sense that we fear He might do us harm, but we should have a respectful fear realizing that He has all power, knows everything, and is everywhere all the time. God sees and is fully aware of everything we do. He sees what is behind and what is ahead, all the threats, all the dangers. There is no place we can go to hide from Him, as these scriptures teach us:

> If I go up to the heavens, you are there; if I make my bed in the depths, you are there. If I rise on the wings of the dawn, if I settle on the far side of the sea, even there your hand will guide me, your right hand will hold me fast. If I say, "Surely the darkness will hide me and the light become night around me," even the darkness will not be dark to you; the night will shine like the day, for darkness is as light to you.
>
> Psalm 139:8–12

> The eyes of the Lord are everywhere, *keeping watch on the wicked and the good.*
>
> Proverbs 15:3 (emphasis mine)

God will bring every work into judgment, including every secret thing, whether good or evil.

Ecclesiastes 12:14 NKJV

These Bible verses are worth meditating on because realizing that God sees and knows everything we do helps us to make right choices.

Many people today may think they are hiding from God, but it is impossible to hide from Him. Whatever is hidden in the darkness will one day come out into the light:

There is nothing concealed that will not be disclosed, or hidden that will not be made known. What you have said in the dark will be heard in the daylight, and what you have whispered in the ear in the inner rooms will be proclaimed from the roofs.

Luke 12:2–3

The Word of God is powerful, and it reveals God's will. To know the Word is to know God and Jesus. The

Holy Spirit is also God, and when Jesus ascended to the right hand of God after His resurrection, He sent the Holy Spirit to live in us, and He is our Teacher (John 14:16–17, 26). He teaches us the Word of God and reveals its meaning to us.

Anytime you approach the Word of God, do so with a reverent attitude and realize that it is holy, it is the truth, and it shows you the way to live.

24

❧

God's Word, implanted in our hearts, has the power to save our souls

❧

*Therefore lay aside all filthiness
and overflow of wickedness, and receive
with meekness the implanted word,
which is able to save your souls.*

James 1:21 NKJV

When we believe that Jesus died for us and was raised from the dead, we are saved by the grace of God (Ephesians 2:8). This is also called being born again. Our spirit, which was dead in sin, is made alive in Christ, and we begin our new life in Him. After we are saved, there is still a maturing work to be done in our soul (mind, will, and emotions).

Once we are born again, our names are written in the Lamb's book of Life (Revelation 13:8; 21:27), and we will spend eternity with God. However, God wants us to let Him change us into the image of Jesus Christ so we might follow His ways and represent Him to the world (Romans 8:29; 2 Corinthians 3:18; 5:20).

I was born again when I was nine years old, but I knew nothing about God's Word. After Dave and I were married, when I was twenty-three, we attended church regularly. Although I did hear God's Word at church, much of what I heard was doctrine. Doctrine, of course, is important, but I also needed to learn practical biblical lessons that would confront and correct my behavior. I don't recall hearing messages about my thinking, yet God's Word says that we will never experience God's "good, pleasing and perfect will" unless our mind is renewed according to His Word (Romans 12:2).

God has given us free will, and He wants us to use our free will to choose His will. This requires dying to self, meaning we say no to ourselves and to what we want to do, if necessary, in order to say yes to what God wants us to do. Paul writes: "I have been crucified with Christ and I no longer live, but Christ lives in me. The life I now live in the body, I live by faith in the Son of God, who loved me and gave himself for me" (Galatians 2:20). What did Paul mean? He meant that he no longer lived his life based on what he wanted to do, because he had died to selfishness and instead desired to live in God's will, not his own.

Here's a practical example of what it means to die to self. Suppose I have a strong desire to do something, but I know it is not what God wants me to do. I have a choice to make: Will I follow my own desires, or will I let go of what I want and follow God? The choice is mine, but Jesus says that one way we show our love for Him is to obey Him (John 14:15). Each time I choose God's will over my desires, a little more of my soul is transformed and made available for God's use.

Paul told the Corinthian church that he could not speak to them as mature men and women because they were still babies in Christ (1 Corinthians 3:1). In other words, they were born again (saved), but they had not matured. They were carnal Christians who made decisions based on their mind, will, and emotions, trying to live their Christian lives according to the world's ways. Paul knew this because they were still jealous and envious, and they quarreled and acted as worldly people do. He wanted to give them the solid food of the Word, meaning more mature teachings, but he had to keep giving them milk or simple teachings because they were not ready for solid food (1 Corinthians 3:2–3).

The solid food of God's Word confronts our behavior, whereas the milk of the Word simply tells us of God's love for us and teaches us the basic things He desires to do for us. Anyone can be excited about these blessings, but can we also be excited about no longer living a selfish life and doing the will of God no matter what we want or how we feel? This is an important part of spiritual maturity.

If we obey God's Word, we will experience its

power to save our soul and work in us, so we can grow up in our faith in Christ and become everything we were created to be. I love God's Word and what it does for us. I encourage you not only to read it, but also to obey it.

25

God's Word strengthens us

My soul is weary with sorrow;
strengthen me according to your word.

Psalm 119:28

Sometimes we need to be strengthened physically, and sometimes we need spiritual strength. When we go through difficulty, especially if it lasts a long time, we may become weary and start to weaken in faith, but thankfully, we can pray and ask God to strengthen us. Isaiah 40:31 tells us that if we wait on God, He will renew our strength. To wait on God means to expect, to look for Him to work, and to long for Him to help us.

According to Proverbs 18:14, when a person has a strong spirit, it will sustain them through bodily pain and trouble, but a weak and broken spirit is unbearable (AMPC). It is wise to keep yourself strong spiritually by spending time with God and feeding yourself a steady diet of His Word. Don't wait until you have a problem to try to grow strong. Be prepared ahead of time to face any and all adversity that comes your way.

The apostle Paul said he could do all things through Christ who gave him strength (Philippians 4:13). He was able to have plenty or do without and still be content (Philippians 4:11–12). We need to be spiritually strong because all of life is not easy. We face storms and trials, and we don't always know when they are coming.

There are times when we need to be strengthened because we are burned out. This comes from working too hard without proper rest, or being under stress for too long. The remedy for burnout, along with prayer, is rest. Resting regularly helps avoid burnout, but some of us think we don't have time to rest. David wrote in Psalm 23:2 that the Lord made him "lie down in green pastures." I have found that if I don't get proper rest, eventually God will make me rest. I will become so tired that I just cannot go anymore. This is certainly not the best way to live. I think each time we become excessively tired, it does some damage to our body. If this happens often enough, we may do some permanent physical damage that we will have to deal with for the remainder of our lives.

Don't buy into the lie that you are the only one who can do what needs to be done. God will provide people to help you if you will let them do so. Often, God does strengthen us supernaturally, but we also need to follow His guidelines to rest at least one day out of seven (Exodus 20:8).

*Do not believe you are the only person
who can get things done.*

God's Word strengthens us and instructs us. If we
don't follow the instructions, then we may not receive
the strength we need.

We can also grow weary when the enemy attacks
us. In the Amplified Bible, Classic Edition, Daniel 7:25
indicates that one thing the enemy tries to do is "wear
out the saints of the Most High"—"the saints" are those
who love God and belong to Him. But God promises
to help us when the enemy comes against us: "So do
not fear, for I am with you; do not be dismayed, for
I am your God. I will strengthen you and help you;
I will uphold you with my righteous right hand" (Isaiah 41:10).

Nehemiah 8:10 is another important verse pertaining to strength; basically, it tells us we can have the
joy of the Lord if we will stay happy: "Do not grieve,
for the joy of the Lord is your strength." God's Word
speaks a lot about joy. The apostle Paul has been called

the "apostle of joy" because he wrote about it so much. If Paul could have joy considering everything he went through, we should be able to be joyful also. Here are some of my thoughts on how to maintain joy:

- Do things you enjoy.
- Don't focus on your problems.
- Laugh as often as you possibly can.
- Think about how blessed you are to know Jesus.
- Be thankful and give thanks.
- Do not be anxious about anything. Instead, pray about everything (Philippians 4:6).
- Have variety in your life. Doing the same things without a break for too long can steal your joy.
- Focus on what you have, not on what you don't have.

Another great help when you feel weak and weary is to wait on God. He gives power to the weak and strength to the weary (Isaiah 40:29). When you feel tired, sit for a while in His presence and do nothing but focus on the strength He is pouring into you.

When we are weary and overburdened, Jesus says we should come to Him, receive His rest, and learn how He does things (Matthew 11:28–30). As we study God's Word, we would be wise to pay attention to the ways Jesus handled situations and to follow His example. He always held His peace (stayed calm and composed), and He never tried to avenge Himself when enemies came against Him. When people made false accusations against Him, He didn't even answer His accusers. He lived to please God, not people. Following His example in these and all other things will help us stay strong.

26

ൟ

God's Word melts
the hard heart

ൟ

*A new heart will I give you and a new spirit
will I put within you, and I will take
away the stony heart out of your flesh
and give you a heart of flesh.*

Ezekiel 36:26 AMPC

Many people have a hard heart and are not even aware of it. I had one as a result of being abused during my childhood and then abused during my first marriage. When people are hurt often enough, they may form a hardness around their heart so they will no longer feel the pain when others mistreat them.

However, when we receive Christ as our Savior, He gives us a new heart, and we have to learn how to behave differently than we behaved before we invited Him into our lives. I found that the more I studied God's Word—especially what it says about His love— the more my hard heart melted. As God healed my broken heart and helped me forgive the people who hurt me, I became more sensitive to the pain of others and had a desire to help them when they were hurting.

The condition of your heart is important.

The condition of our heart is important. Proverbs 4:23 says: "Above all else, guard your heart, for everything you do flows from it." A little bitterness or resentment can easily sneak into our heart, and we may feel justified in having it, but it is very dangerous. Anything negative that is left to fester only becomes more and more of a problem. It is like an infected sore that cannot heal until the infection is dealt with.

God's Word teaches us to watch and pray (Luke 21:36; Colossians 4:2), and one area we should be diligent about watching is the attitude of our heart. Satan roams around like a roaring lion seeking whom he may devour (1 Peter 5:8). We are told to resist him at his onset (1 Peter 5:9 AMPC). As soon as you sense that something ungodly is in your heart attitude, deal with it right away. Go to God in prayer, ask for His help with that situation, and study His Word, letting it strengthen you to deal with the problem.

Here are several ways a hard heart can affect us:

- We find it difficult to have compassion for those who are hurting.
- We struggle to obey God.
- We have a difficult time hearing from God.
- We are often rude to others.

- We may be suspicious of the actions of others instead of believing the best of them, as God's Word instructs (1 Corinthians 13:7 AMPC).
- We find it difficult to simply believe God's Word.
- We struggle to have simple childlike faith.

If you have a hard heart, admit it to yourself and to God. Realize that He has given you a new heart; ask Him to help you learn how to live by it. Study everything you can find in His Word about the heart. For example, Mark 6:52 says that the disciples didn't "understand [the teaching and meaning of the miracle of] the loaves" of bread (AMPC) because their hearts were hardened. They had just watched Jesus feed five thousand people with five loaves of bread and two fish and then gathered twelve basketfuls of leftovers (Mark 6:30–44); yet, when He came to them walking on the water, they were terrified (Mark 6:45–50). They had seen Him work a miracle, yet because of the hardness of their hearts they were still afraid. They did not yet believe that with Jesus all things are possible (Matthew 19:26).

A good prayer to pray pertaining to the heart is based on Psalm 51:10: "Create in me a clean heart, O God; and renew a right spirit within me" (KJV). The heart and the mind are often interchangeable when translated in the Bible. As we learn to think like God thinks, our minds are renewed and any hardness in our heart melts. Keep a tender heart toward God so He can use you in His Kingdom work.

Keep a tender heart toward God.

27

God's Word often brings persecution

But since they have no root, they last only a short time. When trouble or persecution comes because of the word, they quickly fall away.

Mark 4:17

When we receive God's Word, we grow spiritually, and this improves our behavior. Satan
hates our spiritual growth and obedience to God, and
he does all he can do to prevent it. He brings persecution because of the Word, hoping we will give up and
think serving God is just too hard.

Jesus says in a passage of Scripture commonly
called the Beatitudes that we are blessed when we are
persecuted for doing what is right:

> Blessed are those who are persecuted because
> of righteousness, for theirs is the kingdom of
> heaven. Blessed are you when people insult you,
> persecute you and falsely say all kinds of evil
> against you because of me. Rejoice and be glad,
> because great is your reward in heaven, for in
> the same way they persecuted the prophets who
> were before you.
>
> Matthew 5:10–12

We may not feel blessed when we are being persecuted, but Jesus says we are. If we endure difficulties
patiently, He will help us overcome them and reward

us. The persecution we face in the Western world is nothing compared to the persecution believers experience in some other countries, and it doesn't even come close to how the early apostles and disciples were persecuted.

Most of our persecution in the Western world amounts to being made fun of or being rejected. We may miss out on a promotion at work because we won't lie or cheat. Friends may no longer want to spend time with us because we seek to make godly choices and they don't. If this is the case, then they were never true friends at all.

Years ago, when God called me into ministry, it was unusual for women to teach God's Word except to children. I went to a church where people didn't believe women should teach, and they gave me two choices: either I could stop teaching, or I could leave that church. By God's grace, I chose to follow Him rather than the people, and it was a painful, lonely experience. It was hard for me to know that people who I thought were my friends were talking unkindly about me. That church also had a school, which our children attended, and Dave and I soon realized we would have to find a new school for them. In addition, our entire social life had revolved around the church, and that was no longer the case. We lost friends and even family members who thought we were making the wrong decisions as I began to teach God's Word. All of this meant that we had to make many adjustments in a short period of time.

At that time, I had no proof that God was really calling me into ministry. I believed He was, and I was teaching a small Bible study in my home on Tuesday evenings, but there weren't any other opportunities for me at that time. I had a big vision, but only a little was happening. Those were testing years for me, and at times it was hard not to give up, but thank God He gave me the grace to keep going. And today, we have the privilege of ministering all over the world.

I want to encourage you to follow God even if you are persecuted for doing so. The truth is that the persecution we experience in this life is nothing compared to the glory we will experience when Jesus returns (Romans 8:18; 1 Peter 4:12–14).

Let this scripture comfort and encourage you:

But even if you should suffer for what is right,
you are blessed. Do not fear their threats; do not
be frightened.

1 Peter 3:14

Persevering through persecution builds character
in us. Jesus went through it and came out victorious,
and so will we with His help.

28

❧

God's Word transforms us into His image

❧

And we all, who with unveiled faces contemplate
the Lord's glory, are being transformed
into his image with ever-increasing glory,
which comes from the Lord, who is the Spirit.

2 Corinthians 3:18

The Word of God renews our minds, and as we learn to think differently, we begin to behave differently. Romans 12:2 says: "Do not conform to the pattern of this world, but be transformed by the renewing of your mind. Then you will be able to test and approve what God's will is—his good, pleasing and perfect will."

God's Word changes you into
the image of Jesus Christ.

Over time, God's Word changes us into the image of Jesus Christ. This transformation is a process, and it isn't all easy, but it is well worth it in the end. God's Word is truth (John 17:17), and truth makes us free:

Jesus said, "If you hold to my teaching, you are really my disciples. Then you will know the truth, and the truth will set you free."

John 8:31–32

God's Word is filled with grace and truth, and those two things change us. We all need to change and will be changing little by little until Jesus returns to earth.

When I first began to study God's Word, I had so many problems in my personality that it almost seemed impossible for me to ever change enough to be suitable for ministry, but God did change me. After five years of Bible study and learning how to cooperate with the Holy Spirit, I felt I had not changed at all, but of course I had. Satan wants to constantly show us everything that is still wrong with us, but God sees us as we are in Christ and views us as right with Him even while we are still changing (2 Corinthians 5:21).

I want to encourage you not to become discouraged if the changes you need to make take more time than you think they should. The apostle Paul writes:

And I am sure of this, that he who began a good work in you will bring it to completion at the day of Jesus Christ.

Philippians 1:6 ESV

The worst mistake we make as God transforms us and helps us grow is trying to change ourselves through our human effort without asking for God's help. It is the Holy Spirit who changes us, and He uses God's Word to do it. I wasted a lot of precious time trying to change myself. For example, I often said things that got me in trouble. I tried so hard to keep quiet, and it never worked. According to James 3:8, no one can tame the tongue; we need God's help to do that. Ask God to help you think before you speak and then speak words of life, because "death and life are in the power of the tongue" (Proverbs 18:21 AMPC).

I urge you to be pliable and moldable in God's hands. Don't stubbornly hold on to things He is prompting you to let go of. Everything God asks us to do or not do is for our benefit. He is always and only trying to help us. Surrender all of yourself to Him for His use, as Paul exhorts in Romans 12:1: "I appeal to you therefore, brothers, by the mercies of God, to present your bodies as a living sacrifice, holy and acceptable to God, which is your spiritual worship" (ESV).

Don't hold on to things God
wants you to let go.

God loves you very much. He will never love you
any more or any less than He does at this very moment.
His love is not based on what you do, but on who He
is. He is love. You cannot earn love, because it is a gift.
The more you receive God's love, the more it will make
you want to change, but you will change because you
love God, not in order to get Him to love you.

29

☙

God's Word is
a weapon against
the devil, and it is
armor that protects
us in warfare

☙

Take the helmet of salvation and the sword
of the Spirit, which is the word of God.

Ephesians 6:17

We have an enemy, the devil (Satan). He lies to us, hoping to deceive us, and he attacks us in various ways, usually through our circumstances, trying to discourage us. In Ephesians 6:11 and Ephesians 6:13, the apostle Paul teaches us to "put on the full armor of God," which He has given to us (Ephesians 6:10–17).

Armor protects us in battle. The six pieces of spiritual armor mentioned in Ephesians 6 are

1. The belt of truth (v. 14)
2. The breastplate of righteousness (v. 14)
3. The shoes of peace (v. 15)
4. The shield of faith (v. 16)
5. The helmet of salvation (v. 17)
6. The sword of the Spirit (v. 17)

Let's look at a few of these pieces of armor individually.

SHOES OF PEACE

Notice that we have in our armor the shoes of peace. "Shoes of peace" are not mentioned specifically in some

Bible translations. We refer to them as shoes because Ephesians 6:15 says, "And having shod your feet in preparation [to face the enemy with the firm-footed stability, the promptness, and the readiness produced by the good news] of the Gospel of peace" (AMPC).

Romans 16:20 says that the God of peace will soon crush Satan under our feet. When the devil is doing everything he can do to upset you and you hold on to your peace, there is absolutely nothing else he can do.

> And do not [for a moment] be frightened or intimidated in anything by your opponents and adversaries, for such [constancy and fear-lessness] will be a clear sign (proof and seal) to them of [their impending] destruction, but [a sure token and evidence] of your deliverance and salvation, and that from God.
>
> Philippians 1:28 AMPC

Satan works his way into our lives through fear, but God tells us over and over to fear not because He is with us (Isaiah 41:10). We open the door for God to work through faith, so when fear knocks on your door, answer with faith and you will have the victory every time. Also, staying peaceful gives you power.

Staying peaceful gives you power.

THE HELMET OF SALVATION

Notice also that God gives us the helmet of salvation. This protects your mind. The mind is the battlefield on which Satan plants lies, hoping we will believe them. Our mind must be renewed so we will learn to think according to God's Word. When we do, we will not be conformed to the world but will be transformed by learning and believing God's Word (Romans 12:2).

THE SWORD OF THE SPIRIT

A piece of armor that deals directly with God's Word is "the sword of the Spirit, which is the word of God" (Ephesians 6:17). To wield (use) the sword when we are in a spiritual battle means to declare the Word.

When the devil tempted Jesus for forty days in the wilderness, Jesus answered each temptation with the Word of God (Matthew 4:1–11). God's Word is powerful. It is a double-edged sword (Hebrews 4:12) that will protect us and defeat the devil at the same time.

WE HAVE POWER AND AUTHORITY

First John 4:4 tells us that the one who lives in us, meaning Jesus, is greater than the one who is in the world, meaning Satan. Jesus lives in us, and although Satan has power, he does not have more power than Jesus has. God has given us His power and authority over all of Satan's power (Luke 10:19). Please notice that Satan has power, but we have power *and* the authority to use that power. Satan comes like a roaring lion seeking whom he may devour (1 Peter 5:8), but he doesn't have to devour you and me.

Submit yourself to God, resist the devil, and he will flee (James 4:7). We must do the resisting, but God will give us the grace to do it if we lean and rely on Him. Even in your darkest hour, you can stand firm against the attacks of Satan, remembering that you are more than a conqueror through Him who loves you (Romans 8:37).

You are more than a conqueror
through Him who loves you.

30

God's Word
renews our mind

I have stored up your word in my heart,
that I might not sin against you.

Psalm 119:11 ESV

Studying God's Word teaches us how to think properly, meaning to think like God thinks. It teaches
us God's will and keeps us from sinning. If we want
to have what God wants us to have and to do and be
what He wants us to do and be, we must learn to think
as He does. Our thoughts are of primary importance
because as we think in our heart, so are we (Proverbs
23:7 AMPC). I like to say, "Where the mind goes the
man follows."

Romans 12:2 (AMPC) says:

Do not be conformed to this world (this age),
[fashioned after and adapted to its exter-
nal, superficial customs], but be transformed
(changed) by the [entire] renewal of your mind
[by its new ideals and its new attitude], so that
you may prove [for yourselves] what is the good
and acceptable and perfect will of God, even the
thing which is good and acceptable and perfect
[in His sight for you].

This scripture tells us plainly that our mind must
be renewed (we must learn a new way of thinking) if

we want to prove (live and enjoy) for ourselves what God's good will is for us.

My life has been completely changed. This has happened through reading God's Word, studying it, meditating on it, and listening to it. It has taught me the truth, and I no longer believe the lies of the devil. For example, I always believed I would have a second-rate life because of having been sexually abused by my father. But God's Word has taught me that I can let go of the past and press toward the good things that God has for me (Philippians 3:13–14). We are to forget the former things (Isaiah 43:18), because when we are born again, we become new creatures in Christ and all things are made new (2 Corinthians 5:17). Not only did I *not* have a low-rate life, but I believe that God redeemed my life even more powerfully because of the abuse. I believe this because God works all things for our good if we love Him and want His will (Romans 8:28).

I did ask God to get me out of the abusive situation. He did not do that, but He did get me *through* it, and I gained experience that now allows me to help others who have been abused in any way. I personally know the healing power of God's Word.

Any time you spend in God's Word is never wasted. Remember, Scripture instructs us to meditate on His Word (Joshua 1:8). This is a process that takes time, so be patient and keep at it until you have victory. As of the writing of this book, I have been studying God's Word for forty-five years. I still do so every day and will continue to do so as long as I live.

Time spent in God's Word is never wasted.

Colossians 3:2 teaches us to set our mind on things above, not on the things of this world. In the Amplified Bible, Classic Edition, this verse says: "And set your minds *and keep them set* on what is above (the higher things), not on the things that are on the earth" (italics mine). To keep your mind set means to make a firm decision and stick to it.

My husband, Dave, loves to play golf, and I once asked him how it would affect him if he ever reaches the point where he cannot play. He said, "I have already set my mind that if that happens, I will enjoy my life anyway."

Some people think, *If I don't have this or that, there is no way I can enjoy life*. But such thinking is a lie from the devil. We can have the proper attitude toward whatever may happen in our lives by setting our mind in the right direction. I encourage you to renew your mind and attitudes daily. Godly thoughts produce godly actions, and godly actions produce a life that is worth living and can be enjoyed.

Godly thoughts and actions produce
a life worth living.

31

୬

God's Word destroys mental strongholds and teaches us the truth

ৡ

The weapons we fight with are not the weapons of the world. On the contrary, they have divine power to demolish strongholds. We demolish arguments and every pretension that sets itself up against the knowledge of God, and we take captive every thought to make it obedient to Christ.

2 Corinthians 10:4–5

Paul mentions that our spiritual weapons have "divine power to demolish strongholds" (2 Corinthians 10:4). A mental stronghold is an area of our thinking that is entirely wrong due to lies the devil has told us and we have believed. It is an area that Satan has taken over. When we believe a lie, we become deceived, and deception is the main tool the enemy uses to keep us out of God's good will for our lives. Even though something we believe may not be true, it becomes true for us because we believe it.

God's Word teaches us truth and tears down the strongholds the enemy has built in our minds. Once we know the truth, we will recognize lies, and we can take the ungodly thoughts captive and think in ways that obey God's Word. For many years, the idea that I could choose my thoughts never occurred to me. I simply thought whatever came to my mind—and most of those thoughts were provoked by the devil. I believed all kinds of wrong things about God, myself, other people, and my future.

The devil is a liar and the father of lies (John 8:44). Satan will tell us that bad things are good for us, and after he tempts us to sin, he will make us feel guilty for doing it. The longer the earth survives, the greater deception becomes. In our present day, I am seeing deception to a degree I never thought I would see. People believe things that make no sense at all. None of us know what the truth really is unless we know God's Word. His Word is truth, and His Spirit is the Spirit of truth, who comes to live in us to teach us truth (John 14:16–17; 16:13). I know God's Word is truth because I have applied it and it works.

Compare what you believe about God, yourself, other people, and your future with what God's Word says, and you will begin to uncover lies that may have been making you miserable and holding you back from the wonderful life that God has given you through Christ. No matter how many mistakes you have made, God still has a good plan for you. He loves you unconditionally, and all your sins are forgiven if you will admit them, be willing to turn away from them, and live according to God's will.

God has a good plan for you.

My father was an angry man, and any little mistake I made caused him to become angry with me. I came to believe God was the same way, and I suffered terribly with the fear that God was angry with me. However, the truth set me free. Jesus said, "If you hold to my teaching, you are really my disciples. Then you will know the truth, and the truth will set you free" (John 8:31–32).

Jesus also said, "I am the way and the truth and the life. No one comes to the Father except through me" (John 14:6). A lot of people believe there are many ways to God, yet Jesus says He is the only way.

Some people believe their good works will make them right with God, but God's Word teaches that we are saved by grace through faith, not based on anything we can do (Ephesians 2:8–9). We will be rewarded for the good works we do, but our right standing with God is not based on them—it is based on faith in Christ and nothing else. If we have true faith, then we will want to do good works, and our motives for doing them will be pure.

Be committed to studying God's Word, remembering that it is the only truth that exists. Compare all your beliefs with God's Word, and if they don't agree with it, change your mind to agree with what God says.

32

✌

God's Word divides soul and spirit

✌

For the word of God is alive and active.
Sharper than any double-edged sword,
it penetrates even to dividing soul and spirit,
joints and marrow; it judges the thoughts
and attitudes of the heart.

Hebrews 4:12

We are tri-part beings: each of us has a body, a soul, and a spirit (1 Thessalonians 5:23). When we are born again, God comes to live inside of us by His Spirit, and He gives us every good thing we need to follow His guidance and enjoy peace, joy, and right standing with Him. God's Spirit gives us strength, abilities, love, joy, peace, patience, humility, self-control, and many other good things (Galatians 5:22–23). If we follow the Holy Spirit's guidance at all times, we will live in perfect obedience to God's Word.

In addition to our body and our human spirit, we also have a soul, which is comprised of our mind, will, and emotions. Our words are rooted in our soul (heart), and our soul and body make up the flesh. According to Galatians 5:17, the flesh wars against the spirit and the spirit wars against the flesh. They are continually antagonistic toward one another: "For the flesh desires what is contrary to the Spirit, and the Spirit what is contrary to the flesh. They are in conflict with each other, so that you are not to do whatever you want." The *Berean Study Bible* says that the flesh "craves" what is contrary to the spirit. If we want to obey God, the devil uses our flesh to try to draw us into disobeying Him.

The problem we often run into is not being able to discern whether what we want to do is coming out of the soul or the spirit. We ask ourselves, "Is this what I want, or is it what God wants?" The more we learn of God's Word, the easier it becomes to distinguish between the two, but it is a learning process that takes time. If we know and live by God's Word, we will walk according to the Spirit.

When we begin our new life with Christ, our flesh is stronger than our newly born-again spirit. But as we feed our spirit with God's Word, it gains strength and eventually becomes stronger than the flesh.

Let me give you a practical example. Yesterday I wanted to go exercise, but at the same time I didn't want to go exercise. I knew I should go and that exercising would be best for me. I wanted what was best for me, but at the same time I didn't want to do it. My spirit was leading me to do what was good for me and would keep me healthy, give me energy, and make me feel good. But my flesh is lazy and didn't want to get out of the comfortable recliner I was sitting in. I had a decision to make: Would I follow my flesh or my spirit? Thankfully, I finally did go exercise but only because I understood the battle raging inside of me. I knew it was a fight between my flesh and my spirit, and I know enough of God's Word to be able to discern between the two and choose to do what is best.

Here's another example. Let's say someone offends you. You would love to yell at them and let them know you are angry with them, yet, at the same time, you know you should forgive them, as God's Word teaches. You have a decision to make. Will you follow the flesh or the spirit? Issues such as these come up continually in our lives, and the only thing that will keep us making right decisions is studying the Word of God. It is the food we need to keep our spirit strong, and it teaches us about right and wrong, good and evil, wisdom and foolishness, soul and spirit.

Everything God tells us to do or not to do in His Word is for our good, and following the guidance of the Spirit will lead us into the best life possible.

Hebrews 4:12 mentions that the Word divides joints and marrow, which are very difficult to divide. This is merely a metaphor to communicate how sharp God's Word is and how difficult dividing soul and

spirit is. It would be impossible to do without an accurate knowledge of God's Word.

God's Word has changed me and changed my life,
and I look forward to the good changes that will continue to take place as I learn more and more of God's
good Word. I am also excited about the changes you
will have as you apply His Word to your life.

33

❧

God's Word comforts and consoles us

❧

My comfort in my suffering is this:
Your promise preserves my life.

Psalm 119:50

When you are hurting and need comfort, the best and first course of action is to pray and ask God to comfort you. He is the God of all comfort:

> Praise be to the God and Father of our Lord Jesus Christ, the Father of compassion and the God of all comfort, who comforts us in all our troubles, so that we can comfort those in any trouble with the comfort we ourselves receive from God.
>
> 2 Corinthians 1:3–4

God comforts us in all our difficulties, and this enables us to comfort others who may be hurting.

✓ *God's comfort enables you to comfort others.*

I have had my share of injustice, physical pain, rejection, disappointment, and difficult circumstances, and perhaps you have too. During these situations, one Scripture passage that has given me comfort and hope is Isaiah 61:1–7. My paraphrase of this passage is as follows: Jesus came to heal the brokenhearted, to set captives free, to comfort all who mourn, to give us beauty instead of ashes, to give us the oil of joy for mourning, and to give us the garment of praise for the spirit of heaviness. He promises to give us a double recompense (reward) for our former shame and trouble, because He is a God of justice.

I can't tell you how many times I have turned to this passage when I have been hurting or felt discouraged. It has never failed to give me strength and hope. When we are hurting, we need hope that things will change. To hope means to confidently expect something good to happen as we wait on the Lord. The devil wants us to be depressed and hopeless, negative and downtrodden, but God gives us hope and comfort in all our troubles. His grace is sufficient to get us through any difficulty we face (2 Corinthians 12:9).

The Word of God comforts us because it lets us know that God will not fail us and that we don't need to fear. Here are a few scriptures I believe will comfort you:

So do not fear, for I am with you; do not be
dismayed, for I am your God. I will strengthen
you and help you; I will uphold you with my
righteous right hand.

Isaiah 41:10

The Lord himself goes before you and will be
with you; he will never leave you nor forsake
you. Do not be afraid; do not be discouraged.

Deuteronomy 31:8

Even though I walk through the darkest valley,
I will fear no evil, for you are with me; your rod
and your staff, they comfort me.

Psalm 23:4

One of my very favorites, which I go to often, is
Philippians 4:6–7:

Do not be anxious about anything, but in every
situation, by prayer and petition, with thanksgiving, present your requests to God. And the

peace of God, which transcends all understanding, will guard your hearts and your minds in Christ Jesus.

Even though I know Philippians 4:6–7 well and could repeat it without looking at it, I often open my Bible to it and receive comfort from reading it slowly and soaking in the encouraging message it brings.

When we need comfort and go to God's Word to get it, we should read it slowly and let the words soak into our soul. God's Word is like medicine for our soul, and it will comfort and heal us. Quickly reading through a few scriptures may not be very helpful. Spend time in the Word, let the words sink deeply into your heart, and believe God will do what He promises to do.

I have seen God comfort people who were in situations that were so terrible I didn't know how they could get through them, and yet they had a supernatural peace and comfort that can come only from God.

34

God's Word helps us see the error of our ways and turn in God's direction

I have considered my ways and have turned my steps to your statutes. I will hasten and not delay to obey your commands.

Psalm 119:59–60

The Word of God teaches us right from wrong and gives us the grace to make godly decisions. His Word urges us to obey His commands, but we have free choice, and each choice we make affects our lives positively or negatively.

Romans 5:19 is a powerful scripture that I really want you to understand: "For just as through the disobedience of the one man the many were made sinners, so also through the obedience of the one man the many will be made righteous."

This verse teaches us that through Adam's sin, many people became sinners, but through Christ's obedience, many people have been made right with God. It is amazing the positive or negative effect one person can have on others.

You have only one life to live and one life to give. What will you do with yours? I urge you not to be a Christian who merely goes to church once a week, says a little prayer each day, and perhaps reads one chapter in the Bible out of a sense of obligation and then goes out into the world and lives in a way that has no positive impact on anyone else. Be a Christian who fully surrenders to God and seeks to obey Him in all your ways. Ask Him to use you as a witness for Him by living a life that will make others want what you have.

God's Word teaches us that if we obey His commands, we will prosper in all we put our hands to do (1 Kings 2:3; Deuteronomy 5:33). God's will is for us to be in good health and prosper as our soul prospers (3 John 2). Prosperity is not simply about having money. God wants us to prosper in our soul—to have spiritual maturity, peace, joy, righteousness, and renewed minds and attitudes. God wants us to succeed in all areas of our life. We can do this if we know and obey His commands.

We do not have to want to do something in order to do it. Jesus didn't want to go to the cross. We know this because He asked God three times to remove the cup from Him if possible (Matthew 26:39–44). But He also said to His Father, "May your will be done" (Matthew 26:42). He didn't want to go to the cross because He knew how difficult it would be, but He wanted to obey His Father and pay for our sins even more than He didn't want to suffer. This is the place we need to reach also. We need to be willing to do what God commands whether we want to do it or not. When we do what is right when it feels wrong or when it hurts, we grow spiritually.

The rewards of obedience are wonderful. One of those rewards is the peace we have in knowing we have done the right thing. There is no harder pillow to lie on at night than a guilty conscience because we know we have disobeyed God that day.

The rewards of obedience are wonderful.

We all make mistakes, we all sin, and we all have times when we fail to obey God. But thankfully, if we are truly sorry, we can repent, receive forgiveness, and start fresh. God's mercy is new every morning (Lamentations 3:22–23).

We may not always understand God's ways, but if we follow His guidance we will see that His ways work. What you don't understand now may make perfect sense to you later on.

Proverbs 3:5–6 says: "Trust in the Lord with all your heart and lean not on your own understanding;

in all your ways submit to him, and he will make your paths straight."

In order to be obedient to God, we must trust Him. Believe that He is good and that He always does what is for your benefit.

35

God's Word causes us to have joy even in the midst of our trouble and anguish

When I was upset and beside myself,
you calmed me down and cheered me up.

Psalm 94:19 MSG

When I am upset, I can go to God's Word, and by reading it or listening to it, I find that it calms my anxious soul. Jesus says all those that are burdened and overwhelmed should come to Him and He will give them rest (Matthew 11:28). The Word of God is medicine for our souls. It is like soothing oil poured on a wound.

The promises of God give us hope for positive change in our lives. We learn as we study the Word that by putting our trust in God's promises, we can see trouble, trials, and even extreme difficulty turn into blessings. God truly does make all things work together for good to those who love Him and are called to His purpose (Romans 8:28).

Not only have I read this in my Bible, but I have experienced it over and over in my life. The apostle James gives us good advice about how to think about our troubles: "Consider it pure joy, my brothers and sisters, whenever you face trials of many kinds, because you know that the testing of your faith produces per-severance" (James 1:2–3).

The way we think determines our level of joy. To consider something joyful means to think of it that way. For example, think *I can be joyful now in the midst of this trial, because I know it will work out well in the end and help me grow in patience and perseverance.*

Perseverance is another word for *patience.* When we are fully patient, we can enjoy ourselves while we wait for God to change our circumstances.

The way you think determines your level of joy.

First Peter 1:6 says: "In all this you greatly rejoice, though now for a little while you may have had to suffer grief in all kinds of trials."

Looking back, we may remember many problems from which we saw no way out. But by trusting the promises in God's Word, we no longer have those problems, because they gave way to the power of our faith in God.

I remember how frightened I was when I was diagnosed with breast cancer. I had surgery, and here I am more than thirty-five years later. I have been cancer-free all that time without needing chemotherapy or radiation. I was broken inside due to the sexual abuse I suffered as a child, but God has given me beauty for ashes and the oil of joy for sadness and depression (Isaiah 61:3).

God's Word has dramatically changed my life. It has renewed my mind and taught me how to think the way God wants me to think. It has taught me truth, and I now recognize the lies of the devil and can resist them. It will do the same for you.

What kind of problems are you facing right now? No matter what they are, the answer to them can be found in God's Word. Ask the Holy Spirit, who is your Teacher and the One who guides you into all truth (1 Corinthians 2:13; John 16:13), to show you how to handle these situations. Follow His guidance, and you will always end up with victory in your life. Let God's promise in 1 Corinthians 15:57 encourage you: "But thanks be to God! He gives us the victory through our Lord Jesus Christ."

God's desire is to bless you in greater ways than you can imagine, but you will also face times of difficulty, trouble, and testing. During those times, it is important for you to keep trusting God and believing the situation will work out for good. God is working in your life right now, and you will see the results in due time.

36

❧

God's Word gives us great peace

❧

Great peace have those who love your law,
and nothing can make them stumble.

Psalm 119:165

Do you love God's Word? If you do, you will find that studying it gives you peace. Jesus left us His peace when He went from earth to heaven (John 14:27), but we still need to seek it, according to 1 Peter 3:11:

> They must turn from evil and do good; they must seek peace and pursue it.

The peaceful are the powerful. Perhaps you have heard the saying "No peace; no power. Know peace; know power." Peace and power go together, and the more peace you have, the more you will enjoy your life.

The peaceful are the powerful.

Jesus is called the Prince of Peace, and as we fellowship with Him and His Word, we will experience peace. I lived for many years without peace. I don't even think I knew what peace was. I grew up in a home that was continually filled with turmoil, and I was so accustomed to unrest that when I first began to experience God's peace, it seemed boring to me. I had lived in turmoil for so long that I didn't know what to do with myself if I wasn't upset about some problem I was having. Peace certainly doesn't seem boring now. I have come to love peace, and I will do anything I need to do in order to have it.

I believe that life is not worth living if we never have peace. There is much in the world that could upset us and cause us to worry and be afraid. But thankfully we have another choice, which is to trust God and the promises in His Word. They will give us peace even in the midst of life's storms.

When I became determined to have peace in all areas of my life—peace with God, peace with myself, and peace with others—I realized I needed to identify the things in my life that the devil uses to steal my peace.

Of course, worry steals our peace. Fear will steal our peace. Other things that can steal our peace include hurrying, getting upset over petty matters that are not worth getting upset over, and fretting over high prices, retirement, what will happen to our children when they grow up, money, job loss, and a thousand other things. Instead of living in anxiety, we can turn every worry into a prayer and watch God work in our lives in amazing ways.

Arguing with other people is certainly a peace-stealer, and one way not to argue with others is being willing to humble yourself, if that is what is required to keep peace. This could mean saying "I'm sorry," even if you don't think the issue at hand is your fault. It could mean being willing to give up your need to be right or relinquishing the chance to have the last word in an argument. There are some things we must hold firmly to even if they do cause temporary upset in a relationship, but many things that we allow to steal our peace do not fit into that category.

I recently had an altercation with someone, and I felt their actions were wrong in the situation. They didn't see it that way, and I realized that if I wanted to keep my peace, I needed to stop trying to convince them they were wrong and quiet myself instead. The next day I was still a little bit angry, and I knew I needed to completely forgive them in order to be obedient to

God and to have my peace totally restored. I couldn't do it by myself, so I started diligently praying that God would give me grace to get over the situation, to no longer be angry, and to be able to forgive completely. I took a long walk, and when I returned home, I was able to let it go and just go on with life.

We should always remember that God is our Vindicator and trust that if we are committed to keeping the peace, He will bring justice into our situations and our lives.

37

❧

God's Word abiding in our hearts makes us victorious over the evil one

❧

I write to you, young men, because you are strong,
and the word of God abides in you,
and you have overcome the evil one.

1 John 2:14 ESV

To *abide* means to live, dwell, and remain. When God's Word lives in us, and when we abide in it and meditate on it regularly, it gives us wisdom and strength to overcome the evil one (the devil). God's Word is filled with power, and it is both a defensive weapon (armor) and an offensive weapon for us to use against the enemy.

Each time the devil tested and tempted Jesus in the wilderness, He answered by saying, "It is written," or "It is said," and then He quoted a scripture to combat the temptation the devil was throwing at Him (Luke 4:1–12).

Sometimes we try to fight the enemy the wrong way. We need to fight him with God's Word. If the devil tells you that you are a loser and nobody loves you, answer with "The Bible says that in Christ, I am a winner in life" (1 John 5:4–5; 1 Corinthians 15:57) and "God loves me unconditionally" (Romans 5:8; 1 John 4:9–10). If the devil tells you to do something that would be disobedient to God's Word, tell him that you serve and obey God and will be steadfastly obedient to His Word.

Satan is a liar, and all he does is lie to us, hoping to deceive us through those lies. You should resist him the moment he attacks your mind. The only way to do this is to know God's Word, and that takes studying it, abiding in it, and meditating on it regularly.

God's Word should be the center of your life.

God's Word should be the center of our lives. We may go to church and hear a sermon or watch a Bible teacher on television, and this is good. But the measure of thought and study we give to the truth we hear is the measure of virtue and knowledge that will come back to us (Mark 4:24 AMPC).

Make a commitment to let the Word of God be part of each day of your life in some way. It may be through reading, hearing, watching, or meditating on it, but if the Word is part of each day, you will be abiding in it and will have power to defeat the evil one.

Let me give you examples of Scripture verses that Satan does not want you to know:

And the God of peace will crush Satan under your feet shortly. The grace of our Lord Jesus Christ be with you. Amen.

Romans 16:20 NKJV

The thief does not come except to steal, and to kill, and to destroy. I have come that they may have life, and that they may have it more abundantly.

John 10:10 NKJV

So the great dragon was cast out, that serpent of old, called the Devil and Satan, who deceives the whole world; he was cast to the earth, and his angels were cast out with him. Then I heard a loud voice saying in heaven, "Now salvation, and strength, and the kingdom of our God, and the power of His Christ have come, for the accuser of our brethren, who accused them before our God day and night, has been cast down. And they overcame him by the blood of the Lamb and by the word of their testimony, and they did not love their lives to the death."

Revelation 12:9–11 NKJV

Be sober, be vigilant; because your adversary the devil walks about like a roaring lion, seeking whom he may devour. Resist him, steadfast in the faith, knowing that the same sufferings are experienced by your brotherhood in the world.

1 Peter 5:8–9 NKJV

You are of God, little children, and have overcome them, because He who is in you is greater than he who is in the world.

1 John 4:4 NKJV

He who sins is of the devil, for the devil has sinned from the beginning. For this purpose the Son of God was manifested, that He might destroy the works of the devil.

1 John 3:8 NKJV

These scriptures and many others like them let us know God has given us victory over the devil, but we do have to exercise our victory by letting the devil know that we know he does not have more power than Jesus, who lives in us.

38

✿

We are born again by God's living and enduring Word

✿

For you have been born again, not of perishable seed, but of imperishable, through the living and enduring word of God.

1 Peter 1:23

Jesus is the Word made flesh who came to dwell among us, and it is He who saves us from our sins (John 1:14; 1 John 4:10). As believers, we are born again, which means our spirit is regenerated by the power and presence of God. You might say that when we are born again, we get to start over. The Bible says that if anyone is born again, he is a new creature altogether, old things pass away, and all things become brand-new (2 Corinthians 5:17).

Just ponder how marvelous it is to be made alive inside by receiving Jesus as our Lord and Savior. I recently heard a woman's testimony that I think describes this well. She had been abused by religious authority in her life. Her mother died when she was born, and when she was four years old, her father thought it would be good for her to have a female influence in her life. He sent her to live in a convent and school for girls. There, she was beaten regularly, sexually abused, kept in dark places, made to go hungry, given laxatives and then beaten if she had a bowel movement, and many other awful things. She grew up hating God and hating Christians. She became a heroin addict and an alcoholic. She made lots of money, but constantly felt empty inside. She bought herself anything she wanted and was married to a man she loved, but still felt empty inside. Finally, the emptiness became so overwhelming that she cried out to God, and He saved her. She and her husband have now pastored a church for thirty-five years.

God is a God of restoration and regeneration. Until we are born again, we feel empty inside. We know something is missing, but we don't know what it is. We all have a God-shaped hole inside of us, and nothing but God can fill it. It can't be filled with fame, fortune, or possessions. People often won't accept Christ until they come to the end of themselves and realize that all their efforts to fix their unhappiness and emptiness do not work. They may have the mistaken idea that being a Christian means following rules and never having any fun again, but that is a totally wrong concept.

Only God can fill the
God-shaped hole inside you.

Becoming a Christian doesn't mean you have to join a religion. It is about having an intimate, personal relationship with God through Jesus Christ. Your worst day with Jesus will be better than your best day ever was without Him.

The imperishable seed that we have in us is Jesus. God lives in us by His Spirit, and we are His home (1 Corinthians 3:16; John 14:23). It is so amazing to realize that God lives in us. We never have to look for Him, because He is in us. The mystery of the ages is that Christ in us is the hope of glory (Colossians 1:27).

God's mercy is new every morning (Lamentations 3:22–23), so if you need a fresh start today, it is available to you. All you need to do is ask.

The life of God that is in you is energizing, and it will help you do whatever you need to do in life, but you need to trust, lean on, and rely on God. You don't have to struggle through life alone, because God is in you and with you at all times. As you go about your day, talk to Him. Tell Him you love Him and that you need Him. Staying connected to God through prayer will keep the life within you stirred up and active.

Think often of God's Word, for it is filled with life and has the answer to all your questions.

39

❧

God's Word is good news, and it endures forever

❧

*After John was put in prison, Jesus went into
Galilee, proclaiming the good news of God.
"The time has come," he said. "The kingdom of God
has come near. Repent and believe the good news!"*

Mark 1:14–15

The Word of God never gets old; it will always remain fresh and powerful. It never changes. The world may change, and people may change, but God's Word never changes. We may rely on it during all seasons of our lives. When this earth passes away, the Word of our Lord will still remain. First Peter 1:25 says: " 'The word of the Lord endures forever.' And this is the word that was preached to you."

The Word of God is more important than I know how to convey to you. It is filled with life and light; it instructs, encourages, and corrects us. When we believe the Word of God and do what it says, we will enjoy a good life. We will have favor with God and with other people, and the things we do will prosper and succeed.

When we believe the Word, our lives will not be trouble-free. Jesus says we will have "tribulation and trials and distress and frustration" while we live in this world, but that we should cheer up (or "be of good cheer") because He has overcome the world (John 16:33 AMPC). Even though we face trouble, the good news is that Jesus is always with us to help us get

through it, and ultimately, He will use it for our good
(Romans 8:28).

In the world, most of the news we hear is bad news.
We hear of murders, wars, lying, cheating, adultery,
divorce, and every kind of evil and wicked thing, but
the gospel of Jesus Christ is good news. In it, we learn
that God loves us unconditionally and has a good plan
for our lives.

Everything about God is good. We have all made
mistakes in the past, but more good news is that we
can let go of what lies behind and look toward the
things that are ahead (Philippians 3:13). God is good,
and His mercy endures forever (Psalm 136:1 NKJV).

Everything about God is good.

The promises in God's Word are activated in our
lives as we believe them. There are thousands of promises in the Bible, and all of them are for you if you
will only believe. First, we believe and then we receive.
There is usually a waiting period between believing

and receiving, and I think this is a time of testing our faith. We receive the promises of God through faith and patience (Hebrews 6:12). If you have been wait-ing a long time to see one of God's promises fulfilled in your life, I encourage you not to give up, because at the right time you will reap (see the answer to your prayers) if you don't give up (Galatians 6:9).

Ask God for big things because
He is a big God.

Let me encourage you to ask God for good things. If people know how to give good gifts to their children, how much more will God give good things to those who ask Him (Matthew 7:11)? We have not because we ask not (James 4:2), and God is able to do more than we can ask for, think of, or imagine (Ephesians 3:20). So ask God for big things because He is a big God. I would rather ask God for a lot and get half of it than ask for a little and get all of it.

In Psalm 23:6, David says that goodness and mercy

would follow him all the days of his life (NKJV). I think we can believe the same thing for ourselves. You may think, *But I don't deserve good things*. And you are right: You don't, and neither do I. But that is what makes it such good news. God is good to us because He is good, not because we are.

40

❧

God's Word contains
self-fulfilling power

❧

For as [surely as] the earth brings forth its shoots,
and as a garden causes what is sown in it
to spring forth, so [surely] the Lord God will
cause rightness and justice and praise
to spring forth before all the nations
[through the self-fulfilling power of His word].
Isaiah 61:11 AMPC

When a farmer plants a seed in the ground, that seed contains the power to reproduce a plant just like the one the seed came from. The seed has self-fulfilling power. All the farmer needs to do is water the seed and keep the weeds from choking the life out of it, and the seed does the rest.

The Word of God functions the same way. It has self-fulfilling power, and when it is planted in our hearts and we water it with our faith and keep the weeds (sin) out of our lives, we will see amazing things develop simply from believing God's Word.

Faith is amazing. It is "the substance of things hoped for, the evidence of things not seen" (Hebrews 11:1 NKJV). God created everything we see in the world from nothing, and He will do the same for His children who believe and trust in His Word.

God had promised Abraham and Sarah that they would have a child from their own bodies. Naturally speaking, this was impossible because Abraham was about one hundred years old and Sarah was beyond childbearing age:

[For Abraham, human reason for] hope being gone, hoped in faith that he should become the father of many nations, as he had been promised, so [numberless] shall your descendants be. He did not weaken in faith when he considered the [utter] impotence of his own body, which was as good as dead because he was about a hundred years old, or [when he considered] the barrenness of Sarah's [deadened] womb. No unbelief or distrust made him waver (doubtingly question) concerning the promise of God, but he grew strong and was empowered by faith as he gave praise and glory to God, fully satisfied and assured that God was able and mighty to keep His word and to do what He had promised.

Romans 4:18–21 AMPC

This Scripture passage is amazing. The same type of faith in God's Word that brought Abraham's promise into reality will also bring ours. Notice that Abraham had no reason to hope, but he hoped anyway. Remember, to hope means to confidently expect something good to happen to you. What are you expecting? Abraham didn't weaken in faith, even when he considered all his circumstances, which made the fulfillment of the promise seem impossible. He was fully assured that God would keep His Word.

Continue in faith, even when everything seems to be against you.

As Abraham continued to believe God's Word, its self-fulfilling power produced what God had promised. We must continue in faith even when everything seems to be against us. There is no circumstance that is able to keep God from doing what He promises to do. If God is for us, then who can be against us (Romans 8:31)?

When we put a tomato seed in the ground, we will get tomatoes, and likewise, when we put our faith in God's Word, we will get what it promises.

Conclusion

I pray that this book has helped you and that you will return to it often when your faith needs to be strengthened or when you need to know what to do in certain situations. Life is full of questions and problems, but God has given us His Word to help us deal with every uncertainty and to lead us in victory through every difficulty.

God created you to be
an overcomer.

    God has created us to be overcomers in this life. His Word tells us in Romans 8:37 that we are more than conquerors through Christ who loves us. You

are the head and not the tail, according to Deuteronomy 28:13. God wants us to be a success, and His
Word says that whatever we do will prosper (Psalm
1:3). Begin to think of yourself as an overcomer, as
someone who is a winner and not a loser. See yourself
as God sees you, and your life will change little by
little.

Many times, when people get busy, they try to find
time to get everything done by reducing the time they
spend in God's Word or by skipping their time with
Him altogether. Often, they think, *God understands how
busy I am. He'll forgive me for not reading the Bible today.*
Of course, God understands how busy life can be, and
He is always forgiving. But this is not the point. The
point is that we hurt ourselves when we do not make
God's Word a priority in our lives.

Let me encourage you to seek the wisdom and
direction you need in God's Word before looking for
it anywhere else. Other sources lack the life-changing,
life-giving power of His Word. Remember that God
does not guarantee or promise to perform anything
but His Word (Jeremiah 1:12).

God's Word is the best and most trustworthy guide for life. It will never fail you. As you read it, study it, meditate on it, and obey it, you will find hope for every situation, answers for every question, and overcoming power for every problem.

Notes

_&_

Unless otherwise noted, Scripture quotations are taken from the Holy Bible, New International Version®, NIV®. Copyright ©1973, 1978, 1984, 2011 by Biblica, Inc.™ Used by permission of Zondervan. All rights reserved worldwide. www.zondervan.com. The "NIV" and "New International Version" are trademarks registered in the United States Patent and Trademark Office by Biblica, Inc.™

Scripture quotations marked AMPC are taken from the Amplified® Bible, Classic Edition. Copyright © 1954, 1958, 1962, 1964, 1965, 1987 by The Lockman Foundation. Used by permission. www.Lockman.org.

Scripture quotations marked NKJV are taken from the New King James Version®. Copyright © 1982 by Thomas Nelson. Used by permission. All rights reserved.

Scripture quotations marked ESV are taken from The Holy Bible, English Standard Version. ESV® Text Edition: 2016. Copyright © 2001 by Crossway Bibles, a publishing ministry of Good News Publishers.

Scripture quotations marked KJV are taken from the King James Version of the Bible.

Scripture quotations marked AMP are taken from the Amplified Bible, Copyright © 2015 by The Lockman Foundation, La Habra, CA 90631. All rights reserved.

Scripture quotations marked MSG are taken from _The Message_, copyright © 1993, 2002, 2018 by Eugene H. Peterson. Used by permission of NavPress. All rights reserved. Represented by Tyndale House Publishers, Inc.

Do you have a real relationship with Jesus?

God loves you! He created you to be a special, unique, one-of-a-kind individual, and He has a specific purpose and plan for your life. And through a personal relationship with your Creator—God—you can discover a way of life that will truly satisfy your soul.

No matter who you are, what you've done, or where you are in your life right now, God's love and grace are greater than your sin—your mistakes. Jesus willingly gave His life so you can receive forgiveness from God and have new life in Him. He's just waiting for you to invite Him to be your Savior and Lord.

If you are ready to commit your life to Jesus and follow Him, all you have to do is ask Him to forgive your sins and give you a fresh start in the life you are meant to live. Begin by praying this prayer . . .

Lord Jesus, thank You for giving Your life
for me and forgiving me of my sins so I can have
a personal relationship with You. I am sincerely
sorry for the mistakes I've made, and I know
I need You to help me live right.

Your Word says in Romans 10:9, "If you declare
with your mouth, 'Jesus is Lord,' and believe in
your heart that God raised him from the dead,
you will be saved" (NIV). I believe You are the Son
of God and confess You as my Savior and Lord.
Take me just as I am, and work in my heart,
making me the person You want me to be.
I want to live for You, Jesus, and I am so grateful
that You are giving me a fresh start in my
new life with You today.
I love You, Jesus!

It's so amazing to know that God loves us so much! He wants to have a deep, intimate relationship with us that grows every day as we spend time with Him in prayer and Bible study. And we want to encourage you in your new life in Christ.

Please visit joycemeyer.org/salvation to request Joyce's book *A New Way of Living*, which is our gift to you. We also have other free resources online to help you make progress in pursuing everything God has for you.

Congratulations on your fresh start in your life in Christ! We hope to hear from you soon.

About the Author

JOYCE MEYER is one of the world's leading practical Bible teachers and a *New York Times* bestselling author. Joyce's books have helped millions of people find hope and restoration through Jesus Christ. Joyce's program, *Enjoying Everyday Life*, is broadcast on television, radio, and online to millions worldwide in over one hundred languages.

Through Joyce Meyer Ministries, Joyce teaches internationally on a number of topics with a particular focus on how the Word of God applies to our everyday lives. Her candid communication style allows her to share openly and practically about her experiences so others can apply what she has learned to their lives.

Joyce has authored more than 140 books, which have been translated into more than 160 languages, and over 39 million of her books have been distributed worldwide. Bestsellers include *Power Thoughts*; *The Confident Woman*; *Look Great, Feel Great*; *Starting Your Day Right*; *Ending Your Day Right*; *Approval Addiction*; *How to Hear from God*; *Beauty for Ashes*; and *Battlefield of the Mind*.

Joyce's passion to help people who are hurting is foundational to the vision of Hand of Hope, the missions arm of Joyce Meyer Ministries. Each year Hand of Hope provides millions of meals for the hungry and malnourished, installs freshwater wells in poor and remote areas, provides critical relief after natural disasters, and offers free medical and dental care to thousands through their hospitals and clinics worldwide. Through Project GRL, women and children are rescued from human trafficking and provided safe places to receive an education, nutritious meals, and the love of God.

JOYCE MEYER MINISTRIES
US & FOREIGN OFFICE ADDRESSES

Joyce Meyer Ministries
P.O. Box 655
Fenton, MO 63026
USA
(636) 349-0303

Joyce Meyer Ministries—Canada
P.O. Box 7700
Vancouver, BC V6B 4E2
Canada
(800) 868-1002

Joyce Meyer Ministries—Australia
Locked Bag 77
Mansfield Delivery Centre
Queensland 4122
Australia
(07) 3349 1200

Joyce Meyer Ministries—England
P.O. Box 1549
Windsor SL4 1GT
United Kingdom
01753 831102

Joyce Meyer Ministries—South Africa
P.O. Box 5
Cape Town 8000
South Africa
(27) 21-701-1056

Joyce Meyer Ministries—Francophonie
29 avenue Maurice Chevalier
77330 Ozoir la Ferriere
France

Joyce Meyer Ministries—Germany
Postfach 761001
22060 Hamburg
Germany
+49 (0)40 / 88 88 4 11 11

Joyce Meyer Ministries—Netherlands
Lorenzlaan 14
7002 HB Doetinchem
+31 657 555 9789

Joyce Meyer Ministries—Russia
P.O. Box 789
Moscow 101000
Russia
+7 (495) 727-14-68

Other Books by Joyce Meyer

100 Inspirational Quotes

100 Ways to Simplify Your Life

21 Ways to Finding Peace and Happiness

The Answer to Anxiety

Any Minute

Approval Addiction

The Approval Fix

Authentically, Uniquely You*

The Battle Belongs to the Lord

Battlefield of the Mind*

Battlefield of the Mind Bible

Battlefield of the Mind for Kids

Battlefield of the Mind for Teens

Battlefield of the Mind Devotional

Battlefield of the Mind New Testament

Be Anxious for Nothing*

Being the Person God Made You to Be

Beauty for Ashes

Change Your Words, Change Your Life

Colossians: A Biblical Study

The Confident Mom

The Confident Woman

The Confident Woman Devotional

Joyce Meyer Spanish Titles

Auténtica y única
(Authentically, Uniquely You)

Belleza en lugar de cenizas
(Beauty for Ashes)

Buena salud, buena vida
(Good Health, Good Life)

Cambia tus palabras, cambia tu vida
(Change Your Words, Change Your Life)

El campo de batalla de la mente
(Battlefield of the Mind)

Cómo envejecer sin avejentarse
(How to Age without Getting Old)

Como formar buenos habitos y romper malos habitos
(Making Good Habits, Breaking Bad Habits)

La conexión de la mente
(The Mind Connection)

Dios no está enojado contigo
(God Is Not Mad at You)

La dosis de aprobación
(The Approval Fix)

Efesios: Comentario biblico
(Ephesians: Biblical Commentary)

Empezando tu día bien
(Starting Your Day Right)

Hágalo con miedo
(Do It Afraid)

Usted puede comenzar de nuevo
(You Can Begin Again)

Viva amando su vida
(Living a Life You Love)

Viva valientemente
(Living Courageously)

Vive por encima de tus sentimientos
(Living beyond Your Feelings)

Books by Dave Meyer

Life Lines

* Study Guide available for this title